A VIEW OF THE *English Interests in India*

A VIEW

OF THE

English Interests in India;

AND AN ACCOUNT OF THE

MILITARY OPERATIONS

IN THE

Southern Parts of the Peninsula,

during the Campaigns of 1782, 1783, and 1784

WILLIAM FULLARTON OF FULLARTON

GYAN

Published by

Gyan Publishing House
5, Ansari Road
Daryaganj, New Delhi-110002
Phone: 011-47034999, 9811692060
E-mail: books@gyanbooks.com

Distribution Network
gyanbooks.com
India, USA, Canada, UK, Australia

ISBN: 978-93-6780-093-5 (PB)

First Published, 1787

2nd Impression 2024

Printed at: Gyan Press, Delhi.

A VIEW OF THE ENGLISH INTERESTS IN INDIA
Author: WILLIAM FULLARTON OF FULLARTON

A
VIEW
OF THE
ENGLISH INTERESTS
IN
INDIA.

A VIEW OF THE *English* Interests in *India*;

AND AN ACCOUNT OF THE

MILITARY OPERATIONS

IN THE

Southern Parts of the Peninsula,

during the Campaigns of 1782, 1783, and 1784.

IN TWO LETTERS;

Addressed to the Right Honourable the Earl of *********,
and to Lord MACARTNEY and the SELECT
COMMITTEE of *Fort St. George*.

BY

WILLIAM FULLARTON of FULLARTON, M.P.
F.R.SS. of London and Edinburgh, and late Commander
of the Southern Army on the Coast of Coromandel.

LONDON:

PRINTED FOR T. CADELL IN THE STRAND; AND
W. CREECH, EDINBURGH.

MDCCLXXXVII.

TO

THE RIGHT HONOURABLE

THE MEMBERS

OF THE

BOARD of CONTROUL.

MY LORDS AND GENTLEMEN,

AS your Right Honourable Board is invested with the controlling power of this country in all matters of Eastern regulation, I take the liberty of inscribing to you the following Account of the Operations of the Southern Forces on the Coast of Coromandel, and a View of the English Interests in that quarter of the Globe.

The

The remarks which I now preſume to lay before you, are the reſult of perſonal obſervation, unbiaſſed by prejudice or partiality; and it will afford me the moſt unfeigned ſatiſfaction, if any thing contained in theſe pages ſhall prove at all deſerving of your conſideration.

I have the honour to be, with great reſpect,

MY LORDS AND GENTLEMEN,

Your moſt obedient

and very faithful Servant,

W. FULLARTON.

ADVERTISEMENT.

IN order that the local descriptions and military operations mentioned in the following Work may be rendered more intelligible, Mr. FADEN, Geographer to His Majesty, has completed a Map of the Southern Provinces of India, from Madras to Cape Comorin, on a large scale, according to the Plans of Colonel Kelly, Captain Wersebe, and other accurate Surveyors.

In this Map, the movements of the Southern army, during the Campaigns of 1782, 1783, and 1784, are faithfully traced, and the errors of former Topographers are carefully corrected.

ADVERTISEMENT

A

VIEW

OF THE

English Interests in *India*.

LETTER I.*

MY LORD,

IT would afford me the greatest satisfaction, if the transactions which have occurred since my departure from England, enabled me to lay before you any information that might prove interesting, and that might tend to evince the sentiments of

* This letter was written on the passage from India to Europe, subsequent to the Letter addressed to Lord Macartney and the Select Committee of Fort St. George.

 respect

reſpect and veneration which impreſs me when I venture to addreſs your Lordſhip.

If the expedition in which my regiment embarked had been ſuffered to purſue its original object, the tenour of our operations might have afforded a narrative not undeſerving your attention; but our after-deſtination againſt the Cape of Good Hope, our progreſs from thence to India, and our ſubſequent proceedings there, furniſh ſo inferior a ſubject of communication, that I ſhould have been unwilling to intrude upon your ſerious engagements, had not the ſtate of our Eaſt India poſſeſſions become an object of general importance to this country.

Although theſe conſiderations and your Lordſhip's goodneſs may incline you to receive indulgently ſuch obſervations as my recent opportunities ſuggeſt on this ſubject, it is far from my intention however to treſpaſs upon your patience, with any detail of particulars relating to myſelf, or to the events that preceded my arrival in the Eaſt, farther than to requeſt your peruſal of the papers inſerted in the Appendix. My chief object is to lay before you an unbiaſſed ſtatement of recent occurrences in India, and of our actual ſituation there.

The principal exertions during the concluding period of the war with Tippoo Sultaun, were made by the forces ſouth of the river Coleroon, which I had the honour to command; and our operations were ſo intimately connected not only with thoſe on the Malabar coaſt, but with all the tranſactions that occurred within the range of hoſtility, that no juſt view could be given of the one, without a correſponding ſtatement of the other.

In my addreſs to the Government of Fort St. George, the diſtreſsful condition in which I found thoſe countries when appointed to the ſouthern command, is faithfully related; the riſe and progreſs of military meaſures in the ſouthern countries, as well as their interruption by a pacification with Tippoo Sultaun, are likewiſe recapitulated; the local miſmanagement and inherent grievances that have reduced our affairs upon the Coaſt to the laſt ſymptoms of decay, are afterwards explained; and my obſervations conclude with ſuggeſting ſuch meaſures of reform as appear indiſpenſable to the preſervation of India.——A copy of that narrative accompanies this Letter, together with ſeveral authentic communications neceſſary to elucidate the ſubject.

You have heard much, my Lord, and read more, of the miſgovernment in India. There have been declamations without end on the peculations of the Company's ſervants,—and acts without number to retrieve,

trieve, if poſſible, the Company's affairs: but theſe declamations have only tended to aſcertain the rhetorical eſtimation due to the perſons who delivered them,—and thoſe acts have too frequently confirmed the evils they were meant to remedy.

In treating of this ſubject it never ſhould be forgotten, that the leading principle of all Eaſtern inſtitutions is permanency; but the principle, or at leaſt the practice, of all Engliſh politics in India, has been productive of the moſt pernicious inſtability. By the firſt, laws, manners, rites and regulations are handed down from age to age undiminiſhed and unaltered;—by the ſecond, the general order and arrangements of the country are torn aſunder with capricious innovation: and to enforce a ſyſtem ſo deſtructive of the deareſt tenets of the natives, the continued operation of violence is required.

The diſtribution of the Gentoos into Talyngas, Malabars, Marattas, Canaras, and Malleallums, as well as into the different ſects of Bramins, Rajahpoots, Nyars, and into many inferior ſubdiviſions of merchants, labourers, and artificers, has remained inviolate ſince the promulgation of the laws of Brimha, whoſe Shaſter contains the ordinances of their faith, and the pandects of their juriſprudence. Theſe inſtitutes have withſtood the ravages of time, the irruptions of invaders, and the revolutions to which, in all recorded periods, thoſe countries have been expoſed.

The wiſdom of the Mooriſh conquerors of Indoſtan failed not to preſerve this antient fabric of Indian adoration. In fact, the Mahometan governments apparently reverence the rites of the Gentoos, who ſtill conſtitute the maſs of ſubjects on the peninſula. Under the Moors, they are liable to oppreſſions incident to all arbitrary govern-

governments; yet their tyrants have mingled policy with force: and as the Goths adopted the manners of thoſe nations whom they conquered, ſo the Muſſulmen have aſſimilated with the cuſtoms of their Indian ſubjects. They encourage them in huſbandry and manufacture—employ them in their armies—entruſt them with their finance—and, above all, preſerve to them the purity of their Caſts, the ſanctity of their Bramins, and the pomp of their religion. So fully do the Mooriſh princes feel the neceſſity of treating with reſpect thoſe cuſtoms and opinions, for which the moſt timid of Gentoos would ſacrifice his life, that Hyder Ally never failed to make large endowments to the chief temples or pagodas. In 1781, when his army inveſted Tritchinopoly, he waited in perſon on the Bramins of Seringham Pagoda, with a propitiatory acknowledgment to Viſtnou, the tutelary deity of that ſanctuary. By theſe means, in addition to ſuperior talents

 in

in war, and a vigorous adminiſtration in peace, the Moors have extended their dominions over the richeſt parts of the peninſula.

The Portugueſe, on the other hand, whoſe arms and enterpriſe obtained a geographical extent of territory greater than the circuit of the Roman empire in the days of Auguſtus, blindly zealous to propagate the Chriſtian faith, found it eaſier to conquer kingdoms than to ſubvert eſtabliſhed doctrines. By violating the tenets of their ſubjects, they have ceaſed to be accounted among the powers of India.

Happily for the Engliſh intereſts, intolerance in matters of religion has not mingled with our Indian policy. But in our civil and military conduct, intolerance has united with inſtability, to violate the moſt revered inſtitutions, and to force pacific powers into meaſures for our extermination.

mination. So fully are theſe aſſertions verified by every circumſtance attending the origin and growth of our power in India, that on a conviction of our reſtleſs and unſtable views, was founded the policy of the Mogul, the Nizam, the Marattas, and other ſtates of India, who lately aſſociated to accompliſh our deſtruction.

It is not neceſſary for me at preſent to enumerate the various transformations by which the private merchant grew into a powerful ſovereign, with formidable armies, large revenues, rich manufactures, induſtrious ſubjects, and territories more extenſive, populous, and productive than the moſt flouriſhing kingdoms of Europe. My intention is, to convince your Lordſhip that, notwithſtanding the enterpriſe and talents by which various ſubjects of this country have ſignaliſed themſelves during the courſe of Indian operations, no individual efforts

can

can prevent the ſuperſtructure from tottering, while the groundwork is ſo inſecure.

In the earlieſt periods of our aggrandiſement Lord Clive exerted his utmoſt efforts to correct the vices of our Eaſtern ſyſtem. His letters to the Court of Directors recommended an œconomical detail in the departments of public expenditure, a regulated watchfulneſs over the defenſive preparations of the country they had acquired, a conſtant attention to the commercial purpoſes of their inſtitution, a rigid juſtice and inviolable ſecurity to their ſubjects, and a liberal encouragement of induſtry and cultivation. Above all, ſays he, you muſt ſupport a permanent ſyſtem of conciliatory meaſures towards the country powers: for while a doubt exiſts reſpecting your pacific inclinations, their fears will incite them to form machinations to effect your ruin.

Although

Although the current inſtructions from home to the different Preſidencies have been in uniſon with theſe admonitions, our Eaſtern governors avowedly have diſobeyed all orders; they have commenced hoſtility, negotiated for peace, and renewed the war, juſt as ſuited their convenience.

I will not carry you farther back, my Lord, than 1767, when the Government of Madras, after flagrantly offending the Nizam, by occupying the Circars under the pretence of a firmaun or charter from their then dependant the Mogul, ſent a deputation, to ſubmit their claim to the diſcuſſion of the very Nizam who was the injured party in the queſtion; and, without ſatisfying him for the violation, farther than by a huddled compromiſe to pay him a tribute for the Northern Circars, entered into engagements with him to act conjunctly againſt Hyder Ally, then invaded by the Marattas. No ſooner was this union formed,

formed, than it was diſſolved; and the Nizam ſeparating from the Engliſh army under General Smith*, immediately joined Hyder, and continued in hoſtility againſt us; but after ſeveral unſucceſsful engagements, he became weary of the conteſt, and returned with his army to Hyderabad.

The after-narrative of that diſgraceful warfare, as expreſſed in General Smith's letter to Lord Clive, exhibits the moſt ſtriking picture of our Eaſtern councils. There we may learn, by what inverted policy it is poſſible to defeat the beſt-founded expectations; to render abortive the exertions of the ableſt general, and braveſt army;—how an enemy may be reduced, by repeated loſs in battle, to propoſe the moſt favourable terms of accommodation; and yet, thus weakened and exhauſted, how he

* See General Smith's Letter to Lord Clive.

may

may be enabled to triumph over every disaster.

My reference to these facts is only meant to evince, that the contempt which Hyder Ally entertained for our councils, and his enmity towards our establishment, however ruinous to our interests, originated in our aggressions. We had hardly breathed after the war with Hyder, when the public consternation was excited by unprovoked hostility with the Maratta states, against whom, whatever might be the ostensible pretext, I know not of any subject of complaint, excepting that they held possessions on the Malabar coast, extending from the northward of Surat to the vicinity of Goa; while our Presidency of Bombay, exclusive of their island, were circumscribed within the narrow limits of a factory at Surat, and another at Telicherry. Your Lordship has no doubt observed in the printed and

and official communications respecting that contest, a mass of incidents, compared with which, the indignities incurred by the Madras Government in the preceding war of 1767 with Hyder, almost cease to appear disreputable*.

Hostilities at last commencing between the English and French, the English were again involved in war with Hyder Ally. Under these circumstances, it became necessary to consider of a pacification with the Marattas. Negociations were opened; but as we had fought without concert, so we treated without communication. The General negotiates, the Government of Bombay negotiates, the supreme Board negotiates, the Representative of a higher Power negotiates—all differ, all counteract each other; and the Maratta Government found it so impossible to reconcile their contradictory

* See Pechell's account of military affairs at Bombay.

tory propofitions, that they continued the war as the only means of fecurity with fuch unexplicable adverfaries. Long afterwards however, on the eve of our diffolution, as the *fine qua non* of our exiftence in India, they forced us to purchafe peace from them, and to reftore all the poffeffions of which we had robbed them, excepting Salcet; having firft wafted the treafures of Bengal, reduced Bombay to a ftate of infolvency, and expofed our conduct to the whole world, as a lafting monument of perfidy and weaknefs.

We now arrive at the moft eventful period that the Englifh have experienced in Afia, furpaffing every previous misfortune in the iniquity from whence it fprang, and in the calamity with which it was attended. From the date of the difgraceful treaty with Hyder Ally in 1769, till the year 1780, our rulers in the Carnatic feemed to have

have forgotten that he ever had invaded them, or rather that he ever could invade them again. The ſuperior genius of Hyder perceived, that the territories and poſition of the Engliſh, as well as their proficiency in military ſcience, would render them deſirable allies, and give unequivocal ſuperiority to his forces when conjoined with theirs; but experience proved, that he could not rely on men ſo diſunited and unprincipled. To adopt a neutral ſyſtem, neither promiſed ſecurity, nor ſuited his deciſive character. What then remained but hoſtile meaſures, againſt a nation with whom alliance or neutrality appeared alike unſafe?—His campaigns during the preceding war expoſed their vulnerable parts;—their diſregard of military preparation marked out the Carnatic as an inviting field of new acquirement;—and the growing profligacy of each ſucceeding Government, improving on the rapacity

rapacity of that which preceded it, confirmed the hatred which our previous conduct justified *. Hyder's enmity was roused to indignation by our attack on Mahee, a French settlement under his protection: still more was he incensed at the negotiation with Bazalet Jung, brother of the Nizam, and proprietor of Adoni, by which that prince ceded to the English the Guntoor Circar, upon condition that a force should be employed in his defence.

This stipulated force actually marched under Colonel Harper to Inikonda, in its way to Adoni; but in consequence of various procrastinations so many months were wasted, that Hyder had full leisure to post a strong party at the entrance of the pass near Inikonda. The Colonel, finding the enemy in great strength, and that their orders were to attack the English if

* This was the case, until the unalterable rectitude of Lord Macartney checked the progress of venality.

they should attempt to march across Hyder's territory, receded from the enterprise.

Bazalet Jung, on this occasion, experienced the treachery of Europeans; for, relying on our good faith, he had ceded the Guntoor Circar, and afterwards discovered that the movement of the troops towards him was delusive, and that the delays which enabled Hyder to prevent their march to Adoni, were fraudulently contrived by the Madras Government, in order to defeat the performance of their stipulations. On the other hand, had we fulfilled our engagements with Bazalet Jung—had we marched a respectable army to Adoni, such were the advantages of that situation, that while we could have maintained it, no power in India would have ventured an invasion of the Carnatic; for Adoni * menaces Mysore, Beddanore, the countries of the Marattas,

* It is superior, in a topographical point of view, to any interior position in the peninsula.

and

and the Decan, while the natural ſtrength of that fortreſs, and the reſources it commands, ſecure it, if well garriſoned, againſt any danger from a native power: but all theſe conſiderations were ſacrificed—Bazalet Jung was diſpleaſed—the Nizam offended—and Hyder exaſperated.

Every power in India ſaw the danger that threatened the Preſidency of Madras; and the Carnatic was actually over-run by Hyder with an army of 100,000 men, at the very moment when that Government boaſted that he durſt not meditate hoſtility. The melancholy and diſgraceful events that followed, are too unpleaſing to admit of obſervation. The fate of Colonel Baillie's detachment, and the ſubſequent retreat of the army to Madras, are freſh in every memory. After the ſurrender of Arcot and the chief forts to Hyder, he appointed renters—collected the revenues—coined money—and exerciſed all acts of ſovereignty, being *de facto* Nabob of the Car-

 natic.

natic. It is unneceſſary to enlarge on the ſubſequent tranſactions: the arrival of Sir Eyre Coote from Bengal—the junction of a detachment from thence with Colonel Pearſe—the battles of Porto Novo, Pulaloor, and Shulengur, and the other operations of the Carnatic army; or to recapitulate the ſucceſſes of the ſquadron under Sir Edward Hughes*, againſt Negapatam and Trincomaley, which formed the concluding incidents of the year 1781. It is only meant to offer ſome remarks on our political ſituation in thoſe countries, in order to prove the errors of our paſt conduct, and to ſuggeſt what appears to be the leaſt objectionable mode of permanent reform.

* That diſtinguiſhed Admiral exhibited, in the reduction of thoſe important places, the ſame ſuperior conduct which he afterwards diſplayed in his naval actions with the French.

Having had the good fortune to ſerve with my regiment on board the ſquadron during the courſe of thoſe engagements, I cannot mention the name of Sir Edward Hughes, without expreſſing the warmeſt ſentiments of attachment and reſpect, due to ſuch profeſſional merits and ineſtimable private worth.

In

In this ſtage of our diſaſters, the fragments of the Cape expedition arrived at Madras †. It is impoſſible to impreſs your Lordſhip's mind with any adequate repreſentation of the deplorable condition of that Preſidency; nor would it be an agreeable taſk to expatiate on ſuch extremes of human wretchedneſs as were there experienced. If any ſcene of danger and diſtreſs could inſure concord and co-operation among men, the full diſplay of thoſe virtues might have been expected at Madras.

Hyder was in poſſeſſion of the country—Tippoo about this time cut off our ſouthern detachment with Colonel Braithwaite †—the French were landing a body, apparently of ſufficient force to decide the conteſt. In this ſituation, our apprehenſions of the enemy, as well as the deſire of recovering the reputation we had loſt, ſhould have excited us to act with cordial effort; indeed, no proſpect of defence remained, but in the united energy of every individual connected with our cauſe.

† February 1782.

 Under

Under ſuch circumſtances, your Lordſhip will hardly credit the aſſertion, that the buſineſs of the war was by no means the main object of attention. Councils—generals—ſeamen—ſoldiers—and civilians—ſervants of the King, Company, and Nabob, ſeemed almoſt to have forgotten that the enemy were at their gates, and that they had any adverſaries to contend with but each other.

Such pernicious counteractions, at a moment too when the public diſtreſſes ought to have precluded all private contention, excited my ſurpriſe. On tracing the ſource of theſe diſorders, it appeared that they did not originate in any blameable diſpoſition of the parties; on the contrary, the leading characters were diſtinguiſhed by ſuperior talents, and eminent in the different walks of life to which they belonged. From a diſcordant principle in the political part of our Indian ſyſtem aroſe thoſe evils, which were too inveterate to yield to any palliative expedient. Individuals are in a great meaſure out of the queſtion; for the diſunion alluded to, is not the colliſion of one man, or ſet of men, againſt another; it is not of one period, or of one Preſidency; but it is a general contention —a ſhock of ſituations—and a war of departments.

In this critical ſtate of affairs, it was moſt fortunate for the preſervation of our Indian territories, that Lord Macartney had aſſumed the Government of Madras in the preceding June. From the firſt moment, he dedicated his time and talents to reſtrain abuſe, with an undeviating vigour and uprightneſs of intention. Could he have imagined or foreſeen the ruin and diſtraction in which the preceding Governments had involved the eſtabliſhment, it is not probable that he would have left Europe, to adventure on the management of a country ſo overwhelmed by every ſpecies of calamity, that ſuch fortitude, integrity, and perſeverance as he poſſeſſed, could alone have prevented its condition from becoming irretrievable;—but to a mind like his, when once engaged in an important public object, no difficulty could appear unſurmountable, no combination of embarraſſments exceed the reach of his exertions.

In a ſhort time he concluded an arrangement with the Nabob of Arcot, by which the revenues of the countries under his Highneſs's authority were reſcued from miſmanagement, and aſſigned to the Company, in order to ſupport the exigencies of the war.—The ſecurity of Madras, which he found actually experiencing the ſeverities of famine, was provided for with the utmoſt wiſdom and diſpatch.—The inefficient defenſive ſyſtem on which the war had been conducted in the Carna-

tic,

tic, he endeavoured to extend into offensive operations, and every effort was made by the Civil Government to enable the Carnatic army to advance into the enemy's poſſeſſions of Myſore.—The ſiege of Negapatam was undertaken by the direction of the Governor, and proved ſucceſsful, notwithſtanding the oppoſition againſt that meaſure by the Commander in Chief.—Troops were alſo ſent to enable the ſquadron to reduce and garriſon Trincomaley. — The previous extravagance by which the finances of the country had been waſted and public credit overthrown, was reſtrained by a firm and rigid hand. The moſt anxious retrenchment was enforced in every department; not a ſingle malverſation, negligence, or abuſe, ſeemed to eſcape the penetrating obſervation of the Governor; who, at a criſis the moſt diſtreſsful and alarming that the Engliſh had ever

ever experienced ſince their eſtabliſhment in India, exhibited an aſſemblage of talents, energy, and rectitude, of which few examples can be traced in any country*.

In order to account for the riſe and progreſs of theſe diſſenſions, and of that diſcordant principle in which they originated, your Lordſhip will be pleaſed to recollect, that the ſpirit of our primary eſtabliſhment in India knew no power ſuperior to the Company's Government. This authority, perplexed and wavering as it might be rendered by the politics of the different Preſidencies counteracting each other, had

* However ſtrong my inclination is to do juſtice to the merit of Lord Macartney's Government, it would ill become me to attempt a detail of the great and complicated tranſactions in which he was engaged. Deſtitute of materials, and unequal to ſuch an undertaking, it only remains for me to expreſs my hopes that his Lordſhip will be induced to give the Public a hiſtory of the important affairs which he conducted with ſuch diſtinguiſhed ability.

yet

yet somewhat of unity in the idea of its formation; so far at least, that the native powers, considering the Company as the fountain of all English authority in the peninsula, regulated their conduct by such communications as were conveyed through the medium of the Company's representatives. While this prevailed, the Nabob Mahomed Ally, and other native princes in our alliance, conducted themselves with the utmost deference towards the established Government; and though at times they were severely pressed by some rapacious members, they felt a degree of security, and enjoyed an intercourse of good offices, that bordered on prosperity.

The errors of the Company's management having attracted the attention of Administration at home, an act of the legislature was passed in 1773, by which the powers of sovereignty were continued in the Company; but the authority of parlia-

parliament assumed an executive interference in those very powers of sovereignty, by the appointment, recommendation, or confirmation of certain officers of justice, and others to be established in India. The power and dignity of the Crown had, at an earlier period, been brought into direct competition, though not on equal terms, with the power and sovereign authority of the Company. An embassy had been sent immediately from the Crown to the Nabob of Arcot, unavoidably in opposition to the power of the Company. Vehement disputes arose between the Ambassador and the Presidency of Fort St. George. The Governor and Council constituted the regular authority of the settlement, and possessed the powers of administration; while the other claimed superiority as representative of the Sovereign. The Nabob and all the other native princes were perplexed. They had been taught, that in the Company was vested the supreme authority of England, as far as respected

respected India—that no other power had any right of interference there. Now they are told, the Company is nothing more than a private body of merchants, without consequence or consideration in their own country, and who are soon to lose all power and consequence in India.

In this situation of affairs, what shall the unfortunate Nabob believe?—how shall he act?—A host of needy adventurers possess themselves of his confidence, impose upon his credulity, and taint his mind with opinions that have since proved his destruction. "Your Highness (say these adventurers) "must shake off your connections with "those traders;—you must now adhere to "the sovereign power and majesty of Eng-"land:——You, Sir, are an independent "prince; — you are guaranteed in your "territory of the Carnatic by the treaty "of Paris;—the kings of France and "Spain have ratified that treaty, and the "king

" king of England is your protector.—
" Throw off, therefore, all dependence on
" the mercantile association."

You will not be surprised, my Lord, that an Asiatic Prince, who cannot reconcile the contradiction of a body of merchants possessing sovereignty, should have been deceived by language so congenial to his natural propensities; especially when confirmed by the solemnity of public letters, and an embassy from the Sovereign.

From that moment, his attachment to the Company was shaken:—he spoke lightly of their power, disregarded their servants, and counteracted their intentions.

The Government of Madras resented this defection, and forced him to confess that his new allies were either negligent of their promises, or unequal to resist the Company, in whose hands the executive control still remained.

Since

Since that time, the Presidency of Madras has been a continued scene of counteraction. The Senior Officer of the squadron has usually represented his Majesty at the Durbar, and that situation tends to render him, *ex officio*, an object of jealousy to the Company's Government. The Commander in Chief on shore has likewise held an authority from the Crown, so indefinitely expressed, that he could neither submit to the government without incurring professional unpopularity, nor resist without exciting ruinous commotions.

When Sir Eyre Coote assumed the command of the Carnatic army during the administration of Mr. Smith, he had been suffered to engross the whole direction of the war. The succeeding Government found by these means all power and consequence centered in the General. As the Governor and Council of each Presidency, by by the Company's conſtitution, are the delegates of their authority, it ſeemed neceſſary that the Board of Madras ſhould have ſome control over operations for the conduct and reſult of which they ſtood reſponſible to their ſuperiors.—They repreſented theſe circumſtances to the Supreme Board, but ſentence was pronounced againſt them, and the General was confirmed in the unparticipated direction of the war. The movements of the army however did not proſper:—the ſame narrow limits marked their progreſs:—the ſame deficiencies of draught, carriage, and conveyance, as well as of grain and money, ſtill fruſtrated all hopes of profiting by ſucceſs, and defeated every ſuggeſtion of vigorous endeavour.

The Supreme Board, after much acrimonious diſcuſſion, revoked their ſentence, and replaced the controlling power in the hands of the Madras government: but another event ſoon afterwards occurred, which put reconciliation at defiance.—— The Supreme Board determine to reſcind the aſſignment of the Nabob's territory to the Company, and to reſtore his Highneſs to the management of his own country.— They farther reſolve, it is ſaid, to enforce this edict by military power. Sir Eyre Coote is therefore inveſted with full authority for that purpoſe, and on his return to the Coaſt in April 1783, is inſtructed at all events to carry the order into execution. His death, which happened in the ſame month, is ſuppoſed to have prevented much bloodſhed in the ſettlement: for it is underſtood that the General was determined to enforce, and the Government to reſiſt, the order of reſtitution; at a time too, when the country belonged more properly to Hyder and the French, than to either party.

The ſucceeding Commander, General Stuart, was involved in diſcuſſions ſimilar to

 thoſe

those between the Civil Government and Sir Eyre Coote. The campaign under that General against Cuddalore, was interrupted by a cessation of hostility between the English and French. Those dangerous neighbours were thus left in possession of a post, the loss of which would probably have obliged them to abandon India, had not the disunion of the ruling and executive powers distracted our measures, and added a farther proof, that under the influence of discordant principles, neither time nor means, circumstance nor opportunity, can ensure success. The General was superseded in the command of the army, called to the presidency, and afterwards remanded to Europe.

Sir John Burgoyne succeeded as Commander in Chief of the King's troops.—— He asserted powers and privileges that the Government declared to be incompatible with

with the conſtitution of the Company. He perſiſted, and was ſuperſeded by a Colonel on the Company's eſtabliſhment, who, on this occaſion, was raiſed to the rank of Lieutenant General, and Commander in Chief upon the Coaſt. Sir John Burgoyne, in conſequence of this promotion, claimed the excluſive command at leaſt of the King's troops,—and was arreſted.

Another General became ſenior of the King's ſervice, and ſubmitted. The remaining Generals had ſigned a remonſtrance againſt the violation offered to the royal ſervice by the arreſt of their Commanders. Some of them adhered to their declarations, and left the country; others, pliant to the times, enjoyed the benefits of unſerviceable, but not unprofitable, ſtations.—After this detail, your Lordſhip will not be ſurpriſed at any diſturbance that has ſince occurred in thoſe poſſeſſions.

It is not within the limits of my purpoſe to enlarge upon the acts of the legiſlature now exiſting, on thoſe that have been propoſed reſpecting India, or on the proceedings of Parliament in their late capacity as a Court of Inqueſt *.——The pretenſions of Governor and Commander ſtill remain in collision with each other,—the King and Company ſtill continue in that country to be contending powers,—while the Company and Nabob are bound over to perpetual variance. Between the civil and military no line is traced; no redreſs for the latter, no mode of coercion for the former, and the warfare of the Preſidencies is extended and confirmed.

My Letter to the Select Committee of Fort St. George contains every other

* Since this paper was written, the powers of Governor and Commander in Chief have been united in the perſon of Lord Cornwallis, and other important arrangements have taken place for the correction of our Indian ſyſtem.

material

material incident reſpecting the concluding period of the war, the circumſtances under which the peace with Tippoo Sultaun was concluded, and the enumeration of internal evils on the coaſt of Coromandel. In the diſcuſſion of thoſe important particulars, I have not heſitated to ſuggeſt the detail of means by which alone I conceive it poſſible to effect a renovation in the Eaſt. Theſe obſervations on the interior miſgovernment of the country are, in their general tendency, not only applicable to Coromandel, but to the other Preſidencies; and as ſimilar evils operate in each, correſponding remedies muſt be applied to all.

If our condition be deſperate upon the Coaſt, it will appear not leſs deplorable in Bengal; when we conſider that the decline of that Government has advanced with rapid ſtrides during peace, while Madras has ſuffered the devaſtations of war.

 But

But before we enter on a particular view of this melancholy ſubject, it may be neceſſary to ſtate the extent and local circumſtances of our poſſeſſions in that quarter.

The provinces of Bengal, Bahar and Oriſſa, as poſſeſſed by the Britiſh, and including Benares *, contain an area of 162,000 ſquare miles; their annual revenues are ſuppoſed to have amounted, in happier times, to 5,000,000*l.* ſterling, and their population to 11,000,000: the province of Oude and its dependencies comprehend an area of 53,286 ſquare miles, yielded a revenue of 3,500,000*l.* and maintained 20,000,000 of people.

It muſt be obſerved, that the Mogul Government in India was a foreign and oppreſſive government; and conſequently, that the countries under its authority were far from having attained their higheſt period of improvement. It is likewiſe demonſtrable,

* See Major Rennell's Memoirs.

that

that Bengal and the lower parts of the other provinces, being extremely fertile, and chiefly adapted to the cultivation of rice, ought to maintain a greater number of people on an equal ſurface, than any the moſt fertile country where rice will not grow; becauſe rice yields two or three annual crops, and the average of each crop is comparatively greater than that of any other grain. Let us now compare the produce, population, and revenues of theſe countries with thoſe of Great Britain, which, according to Major Reynell, contains an area of 96,400 ſquare miles. The population of Great Britain may amount to 8,000,000, and the preſent revenues are about 14,000,000*l*. By this ſtandard your Lordſhip will be able to judge of the comparative value of the Engliſh poſſeſſions in Bengal; and if to thoſe you add the coaſt of Coromandel, its area being 65,944 ſquare miles, ancient population 9,000,000, and revenue in former times 3,000,000*l*., the aggregate of theſe territories will form a-

 domi-

dominion nearly equal in revenue, and far superior in population as well as in extent, to Great Britain,—to the richest and most productive kingdom, in proportion to its area, that ever existed in the temperate zones.

In former times the Bengal countries were the granary of nations, and the repository of commerce, wealth and manufacture in the East. Vessels from all quarters poured out their treasures on the banks of the Ganges; and the numberless nations that people the northern regions of Indostan, as far as Cashmire, Lahore and Thibet, including a range of several thousand miles, used to deposit their riches there, as the great mart and centre of their traffick. But such has been the restless energy of our misgovernment, that within the short space of twenty years many parts of those countries have been reduced to the appearance of a desert. The fields are no longer cultivated,—extensive tracts are already overgrown with thickets,

thickets,—the husbandman is plundered,—the manufacturer oppressed,—famine has been repeatedly endured,—and depopulation has ensued. The districts are farmed out to Renters, or Zemindars,—and the collections, as well as all other business relating to finance, are committed to a Provincial Chief, who reports to the Committee of Revenue. The Renter holds by a precarious tenure, while it costs him so much to procure and maintain his situation, that if his exactions bear proportion to his risk and advance of money, they must be extremely severe indeed. Neither would it suit the views of a Chief to be less industrious in the business of extortion. They must therefore be unusually inexpert if they do not between them contrive to distress the inhabitants, to ruin agriculture, and to defraud the Government of at least thirty or forty *per cent.* of the stipulated payments. This they manage by statements of approaching want, which they them-

themſelves have occaſioned; by accounts of provincial works, which are never performed; by unjuſtifiable deductions, and by connivance at the defalcations of the managers.

The huſbandmen and Ryots dependent on theſe depredators (compared with whom the feudal Serfs were in a ſtate of freedom) are in their turn happy mortals, when contraſted with the weavers and manufacturers. If the former be plundered of their grain, the chaff at leaſt is left for their ſubſiſtence; but ſuch is the ſyſtem of commercial regulation that the wretched manufacturers have hardly a reſource. The Commercial Chief, to whom they are ſubject, and who, under the Committee of Trade and Manufacture, is charged with the buſineſs of inveſtment, aſſigns to all the portion of their labour,—by a ſmall advance pretends to an appropriation of their induſtry,—denies their right to uſe their ingenuity for their own advantage,—

establishes a ruinous monopoly, by the abuse of power, and treats them as bondsmen toiling for his benefit. The consequence is, desertion among the weavers, a decreasing investment for the Company, enormous acquisition for himself, and a fatal stagnation of all trade and manufacture throughout his district.

In Oude, Rohilcund, and all the upper countries within our influence, the natives are, if possible, still more distressed. Various hordes have been driven to despair by hardship and exaction. They have assembled in formidable force, and menaced the whole country:——the husbandman goes to the plough with a firelock over his shoulder, while the Government is too feeble to restrain these outrages, and too much depressed to afford relief.

If we trust to our military on the Bengal establishment for protection against these alarming

alarming enormities, we ſhall find, that entire corps have exiſted on paper, who, excluſive of the Commandant and Staff, never had any exiſtence but on paper; and it will farther appear, that thoſe Sepoys who have a real exiſtence, are neither well diſciplined, nor regularly paid. The decreaſing produce of the country is conſumed by the utmoſt contrivance of profuſion; and ſo waſteful is the mode of contribution, that the country of Oude, period after period, has fallen into arrears, leaving the exhauſted prince without means of ſupporting his government, or of maintaining his family.

When Lord Clive, by his treaty with Sujah Dowla, reſtored that great country to its rightful owner, ſtipulating only in behalf of the Company forty-ſix lacks of rupees for its military defence *, he meant to proclaim aloud throughout Indoſtan, the

* To pay a brigade which the Company ſtations in the province.

juſtice

justice and moderation of English policy, and to convince the country powers, that the Company rather chose to be friends and protectors, than tyrants and usurpers over those they conquered. Little did that superior genius foresee, that by his boasted treaty the treasures of a powerful prince were indirectly to be transferred into a sinking-fund, and his whole dominions converted into an asylum for the sole use and benefit of prodigals and incorrigibles.

It would be a trespass on your patience, my Lord, to expatiate farther on the impolicy by which a country, superior in wealth and means to the whole kingdom of England, has been so speedily precipitated, without convulsion or internal war, into a state of actual insolvency: neither can I, without impertinence to your Lordship's ready apprehension, enlarge upon the strong suggestions that impress my mind with the impending catastrophe, about to close this scene of unexampled depravity.

But the induſtry of the Supreme Board is by no means confined to Bengal and its adjacent provinces; they have an extended latitude of power: every other board and preſidency is ſubject to their ſway, and their controlling influence pervades the whole politics of India. Without diſcuſſing the merits of this unbounded interference, experience has evinced, that in its preſent modification, it has diſconcerted every meaſure of the other Governments, and ſunk them in the eſtimation of all neighbouring ſtates; while the Supreme Board ſtationary in Calcutta has laboured under ſuch impediments of diſtance, local ignorance and endleſs avocation, that in every inſtance where they have deſcended to ſuch interference, they have expoſed themſelves to public ridicule; and after marring the buſineſs beyond all chance of remedy, have been forced at laſt to throw it from themſelves upon the preſidency, to which from habit, vicinity, and connection it did of right belong.

At

At one time, they propoſe to ſurrender the whole of the northern Circars to the Nizam for a trifle; at another, they diſpatch a negotiator, to offer the rich province of Tinnivelly to the Dutch for leſs than a trifle, for the uſe of one thouſand Dutch mercenaries!—Fortunately, notice of a Dutch war was received, before this extraordinary treaty could be executed, and the negotiator, Mr. Dighton, got no farther than Madras.—But obſerve, my Lord, ſuppoſing the province of Tinnivelly to yield an annual revenue of 250,000*l.* at twenty years purchaſe, the property of it is worth 5,000,000*l.* At this rate did the Supreme Board of India, propoſe to purchaſe the uſe of one thouſand Dutch mercenaries!—You will hardly require any farther illuſtration, that though this ſtationary Board, circumſcribed in the means of intercourſe and information, and overwhelmed in the interior buſineſs of Bengal, cannot eaſily accompliſh any public benefit, by the

latitude

latitude of its control, yet aſſuredly it is enabled to defeat all uſeful views of every other Board, to thwart or over-rule all plans of public ſervice, and, in a paroxyſm of political phrenſy, to make away with half the peninſula.

If it be judged expedient to have a Supreme Board of India, in whom all the controlling powers of Government ſhall ultimately concentrate, in the name of common ſenſe let it be a Board of Circuit;—let it be a Board of inſpection, as well as of control, compoſed of members from each preſidency, detached from the embarraſſments and corruption of provincial regulation:—let it be a Board that can obſerve with impartiality, judge with accuracy, and act with vigour;—that can move to any ſpot in India, where public emergencies are moſt urgent, and call more immediately for its preſence. Thus, and thus only, can it become a Board of extended efficiency either to enforce obedience, restrain subordinate misconduct, or unite in one connected series the vast and complicated mass of Indian affairs*.

Leaving this gloomy retrospect, let us consider how we are situated with regard to other powers, and what we are likely to become on the peninsula. The territories of hither India, or what has inaccurately been called the empire of the Great Mogul, extends 1680 miles in length, 1440 in breadth, contains an area of 1,138,400 square miles, and maintains 110,000,000 of inhabitants. Taking the area of Great Britain and Ireland at Major Reynell's estimate of 131,800 square miles, and 10,000,000 of inhabitants, it is nearly nine

* The preceding remarks on the condition of Bengal and its adjacent territories are not the result of personal observation, and therefore may be considered as less deserving attention than those which I have ventured to offer on the affairs of Coromandel. There is little doubt however, considering the natural fertility of those countries, that a mild and permanent administration might soon restore them to prosperity.

times as extenſive, and contains eleven times as many people as the three kingdoms.

I will not hazard any calculation of the groſs produce and revenue of that empire, but they bear more than a due proportion to this ſuperior population and extent. Its ſoil affords every article for the ſubſiſtence or conveniency of man that can be cultivated in the lower latitudes. It has for ages been the ſeat of manufacture, induſtry, and commerce. Its inhabitants are civiliſed, ingenious and refined, accuſtomed to war, and proficients in the arts, ſciences, and embelliſhments of peace. With ſuch ſuperlative advantages, no ſtate recorded in the annals of Europe could ſtand in competition with the Mogul Empire, if ſuch an empire did in fact include under one government the territories to which it gives a name; but the vaſt tract comprehended under that vague deſcription is parcelled out among a multiplicity of diſcordant powers, and peopled

pled by numberleſs tribes, diſſimilar in manners, language, and religion.

If we divide the whole region into 114 geographical parts, we ſhall find, that of theſe, ſomething leſs than one part belongs to the Mogul and his immediate adherents; to the Affgans, Kaſhmirians, Pitans, Candahars, Seets, Abdallas, and various other northern Hordes, twenty-five parts; to the Maratta States, including Berar, forty-eight; to the Nizam, including Adoni, five and an half; to the Circar of Tippoo Sultaun, including Cudapah, eight and an half; to the Rajah of Travancore, one; to the Engliſh, and their adherents, twenty-eight and an half: the remainder may be aſſigned to the petty Rajahs, Polygars, and other claſſes of aboriginal Gentoos, who have hitherto defied the powers of the creſcent and the croſs, and, under cover of woods, mountains, and inacceſſible retreats, have aſſerted independence.

 Of

Of these, the Travancore Rajah, the Malabar Rajahs, and such of the interior Chiefs as never had the misfortune of our intercourse, have, I believe, no reason to complain of us; but every other individual state has been so deeply injured and insulted by the English, that if their resentments be proportioned to their wrongs, they can scarcely ever be effaced.

When the Bengal Government withdrew their covenanted stipend from the Mogul, and forced him, by their usage, to fly from his residence at Ilhabad, and to throw himself upon the mercy of the contending Chiefs and Hordes who infest the environs of Delhi, they should have recollected that, fallen as he is, and diminished in his splendor, he is still of material consequence in the affairs of India, being the acknowledged paramount of all the Mahometan powers in those countries *.

* His late minister Nidziff Cawn had 60,000 horse under his command.

The Affgans, Pitans, Doranies, Abdallahs, Condahars, Kashmirians, and other hordes of Mussulmen who people the northern territories of Indostan, are brave and warlike, impatient of peace, and eager for adventure. So unsettled is the present state of all those northern countries adjoining to Bengal, that any resolute leader, black or white, of military reputation, might, on the shortest notice, raise an army of 100,000 men, ready to follow him as long as he could feed and pay them. Even in Oude, near 150 lacks of the revenue cannot be collected, but by the aid of a leader, who constantly maintains 10,000 troops and fifty pieces of cannon ready for emergencies.

The Duab* has been twice farmed out to English gentlemen, on condition that they should raise or employ a force sufficient to collect the revenues of it, with permission, after paying the stipulated sum into

* A province near Oude.

the Nabob of Oude's treasury, to plunder and ransack the districts for their own advantage: but of late it has become the receptacle of the rich and disaffected leaders throughout the country, who fortify themselves there, maintain considerable force, and assert a state of open independence. The followers of Nidziff Cawn, and of other great Chiefs, have hitherto been maintained by quartering different bodies of them on particular districts, with orders to the Commander of each body to collect the revenues of the country, and to subsist his troops by force of arms. But by this outrageous system, those countries are already exhausted, and these destroyers, like the Huns and the Visigoths, must seek for subsistence and plunder in new acquisitions.

If they direct their progress towards Bengal*, they will find that country as open to invasion as it was on the day when we

* Bengal is, however, naturally a strong country.

first

first took possession of it:—not a fort, not a barrier, not a post to resist their progress, to the very suburbs of Calcutta.

It would ill become me to offer any suggestions unfavourable to the military upon that establishment. Brave and zealous they undoubtedly are, and would probably defeat their enemies as often as they hazarded a close engagement; but allowing, which is not the fact, that they were neither deficient in Europeans nor in cavalry,—that their Sepoys were in the highest state of discipline, and that the vigor and dispatch of Government, contradicting all former instances, should enable the army to quit their cantonments in the best order on the first notice of invasion; still we are taught, by recent and severe example, that a force constituted on the principle of our Indian armies, without previous well-concerted measures of defence, cannot possibly protect an extended country from the rapid devastations of hostile cavalry. If they should fail in driving us from the provinces, they are at least sure to enrich themselves with spoil, and to render them, like the Carnatic, a possession scarcely worth contending for.

The same observations apply with equal truth to the Maratta states. Their sentiments towards us are not less justly marked with impressions of resentment. They have repeatedly asserted the claim of Chout or tribute from Bengal, which, in their idiom, is nearly synonymous with impending invasion. Their numbers and co-operation, in contrast with our discordant weakness, ensure them an ample crop of laurels, as soon as they shall resolve to pass the Jumna. With regard to the Nizam, our momentary security is founded on his pacific character. Possessed as he is of a great and fertile sovereignty, ample revenues, and an army of 60,000 troops, which

he

he could double with facility on a few months notice, nothing was wanting but determination to have gratified to the full his enmity againſt the Engliſh. When Hyder invaded the Carnatic, the Nizam had only to march a force into the Northern Circars, and thoſe enviable territories muſt infallibly have reverted to their rightful owner.'

But theſe are inferior dangers, when compared with the ſtrength and menacing condition of Myſore. The recent growth and warlike advancement of that ſtate exhibit a phenomenon unparalleled in hiſtory. In the earlier part of this century, when the Delaway or Regent of Myſore marched againſt Tritchinopoly with a great body of horſe, their troops were in the loweſt ſtage of military ignorance; and their unſkilfulneſs was only equalled by their puſillanimity. The country was then governed by a native Rajah, the lineal heir of the Muſnud. He was of the Canara cast, and the great body of his people were likewise of Canara or Gentoo descent. They were happy under his government; but they were neither rich nor respectable.

By the ghauts or mountains, on which the table land of Mysore is elevated, it is separated from the Carnatic on the east, from the great plains of Coimbatore on the south, from the Malabar territories on the west, and from the countries of Beddanore and Ghutty on the north.—These ghauts are only accessible at particular places, and oppose no inconsiderable obstacles to the progress of invaders. The situation of Mysore is remote from habitual interference with adjacent powers; its soil is less fertile than the lower countries that surround it, and its inhabitants were not enriched by commerce and manufacture, nor by these means exposed to their more powerful and industrious neighbours.

bours. Under ſuch circumſtances, it might have enjoyed its primeval tranquility, had not a ſuperior genius effected a ſignal revolution in the affairs of that country.

Hyder Naick, or Hyder Ally, the ſon of a Killidar who commanded a fort of ſome ſtrength on the confines of Myſore, ſoon rendered himſelf ſuperior to all the other commanders in the Myſore ſervice. At the attack of the bloody Choultry on Seringham iſland, mentioned in Mr. Orme's invaluable hiſtory, he particularly diſtinguiſhed himſelf, as well as on every other occaſion in which he either acted or adviſed. Without dwelling on the gradations of his conduct, in attaining confidence and elevation, it is enough to ſay that he roſe to be the prime general and chief miniſter of his maſter. Clothed with the authority of theſe employments, and ſupported by his aſpiring talents, he ſoon left his ſovereign nothing but the name, and

and at laſt doomed him and his whole family to confinement, exhibiting them from time to time in great ſtate, to ſoothe and pleaſe the people, while he in fact transferred the ſceptre to his own hands.—He trained his peaceful ſubjects to the uſe of arms, by new modelling the military ſyſtem; by inviting all ranks of Moormen, Rajapoots, and other warlike caſts, to join his ſtandard; by encouraging or rather alluring French and other Europeans to enter into his ſervice; and above all, by a courſe of ſevere and unremitting duty in the field. He attacked, and ſucceſſively ſubdued the numerous Polygars, Chiefs, and petty Rajahs, whoſe poſſeſſions lay within his reach. He extended his views againſt the countries ſouth of the Ghauts, as far as the confines of Tritchinopoly and Madura, on the Malabar coaſt. He reduced the Zamorin or Sovereign of Calicut, the Rajah of Paligat, the other Malabar Rajahs, and rendered the Rajah of Cochin tribu-

tary

tary to his Circar. He conquered Beddanore, Goutty, and Chitelldroog; the countries of Cudapah, Kanoul, and Savanore; thus extending his dominions as far north as Goa on the Malabar ſea, and acroſs the peninſula to the country of Palnaud and Ganjam, on the coaſt of Coromandel.

With theſe, and other interior acquiſitions, the Rajahſhip of Myſore grew into a powerful ſtate, 400 miles in length from north to ſouth, and near 300 miles in breadth from eaſt to weſt, with a population of many millions; an army of 300,000 men, and 5,000,000*l.* of annual revenue. Theſe atchievements were the reſult of intrepid perſeverance. He next ventured to try his ſtrength with the Marattas and with the Engliſh,—though he could not vanquiſh them, yet he increaſed in ſelf-confidence, and public eſtimation. His very failures he turned to account, and,

and, like Czar Peter, ſubmitted to be worſted, that he might learn to be ſuperior.

During the long interval of peace with the Engliſh, from 1769 to 1780, the improvement of his country, and the ſtricteſt executive adminiſtration, formed the conſtant objects of his care. Under his maſterly control, they attained a perfection never heard of under any other Indian Sovereign; the huſbandman, the manufacturer and the merchant proſpered in every part of his dominions; cultivation increaſed, new manufactures were eſtabliſhed, and wealth flowed into the kingdom. But againſt negligence or malverſation he was inexorable. The Renters, the Tax-gatherers, and other officers of revenue, fulfilled their duty with fear and trembling; for the ſlighteſt defalcation was puniſhed with the chaubuck*, or with death.

* The chaubuck is an inſtrument for ſcourging criminals.

death. He employed ſpies and intelligencers in every corner of his own dominions, and in every court of India; and he had other perſons in pay, who ſerved as checks upon them, and watched all their operations.

The minuteſt circumſtance of detail, the produce of a crop, the cultivation of a diſtrict, the portion paid to the Circar, and that reſerved to the inhabitants, were accurately known to him :—Not a movement in the remoteſt corner could eſcape him,—not a murmur or intention of his neighbours, but flew to him.—It will hardly appear exaggeration to ſay, that he was acquainted wirh every ſpot, and almoſt with every perſon in his empire, when we conſider that he was in a continued round of inſpection.—In his Durbar, during the hours of buſineſs, reports from all corners were received :—his ſecretaries ſucceſſively read to him the whole correſpondence of the day :—

to

to each he dictated in few words the substance of the anſwer to be given; which was immediately written, read to him, and diſpatched.

On his right and left hand, during theſe hours, were placed bags of gold and ſilver; out of which, thoſe who brought him intelligence were rewarded by one or more handfuls of coin, proportioned to their deſerts; he was acceſſible to all: every horſeman or ſepoy, that wanted to enter his ſervice, was inſpected by himſelf; every Jemidar, or officer of any note, was intimately known to him. His troops were amply paid, but not a fraction was loſt. Thoſe who ſupplied his camps, garriſons and cantonments, were all under ſuch contribution, that almoſt the whole military diſburſements reverted to his treaſury. There was no contractor bold enough to hazard a public impoſition. There was no commander ingenious enough to ſcreen inability

inability or disobedience, nor a defaulter that could elude detection. He possessed the happy secret of uniting minuteness of detail with the utmost latitude of thought and enterprise. As his perseverance and dispatch in business were only equalled by his pointedness of information, so his conciseness and decision in the executive departments of a great government, are probably unprecedented in the annals of men. Conscious from experience of his own ability, and of the weakness and distraction of the English, he planned their extirpation from India. He summoned all the native powers to join his cause:—they hesitated. He determined to act alone—and conquered the Carnatic.

His death, in December 1782, left the accomplishment of his farther designs to his son and successor, Tippoo Sultaun, to whom he bequeathed an overflowing trea-

 sury,

ſury, which he had filled,—a powerful empire, which he had created,—and an army of 300,000 men, whom he had formed, diſciplined, and enured to conqueſt.

In my annexed letter to the Board of Madras, the perſpective of events in the concluding period of the war, as well as the circumſtances under which the peace with Tippoo Sultaun was concluded, are faithfully pourtrayed. The ſubſequent proceedings of our adverſary have confirmed the prevalent belief, that the preſent ceſſation is only a ſhort reſpite with a view of afterwards renewing the conteſt, when, through our negligence and his exertion, he may be enabled to attack us with ſuperior advantage. His conduct has not been equivocal:—his contempt of the Engliſh incites him to diſdain evaſion, and his enmity is a conſtant ſtimulus to his hoſtile preparations. In order more effectually

ally to complete his arrangements for driving the Christians out of India, he had hardly signed the treaty with our Commissioners, when he solicited all the great Mahometan powers, the Grand Signior himself not excepted, to contribute their assistance in stores, arms and artificers. He established forges, founderies and armories throughout his dominions,—replenished his magazines, which had been exhausted during the war,—and new-modelled his army on the most efficient footing.

While these arrangements are so formidable as to excite well-grounded apprehensions, his public acts and declarations already ascertain their object and direction. He has claimed and menaced the Guntoor Circar, adjoining to the country of Cudapah. If he should be suffered to take possession of that district, the whole northern Circars will unavoidably be severed from the Presidency, and his dominion be extended over all thoſe valuable provinces. On the other hand, if we reſiſt his aſſumptions, he hoiſts his junda*, and renews the war.——And, under ſome pretence or other, a renewal of the war is unavoidable :—he has ſworn to it.—While we, on our part, muſt wiſh for that event, if we mean to regain our character, or ever to be numbered among the powers of India.

There was a period when peace and forbearance formed the principle, though they never were the practice, of our Indian policy. In thoſe days, inveſtment only was our object, and the increaſe of territorial acquiſition was reprobated by every faithful and enlightened ſervant of the public.——Prove yourſelves juſt,—prove yourſelves moderate,—evince to all India that you are determined to refrain from conqueſt,—was the ſound and earneſt doctrine of Lord Clive to the Directors. Had theſe tenets

* The banners under which Indian armies fight.

been

been adhered to from the first, our establishments in India would have continued peaceful factories;—we should have remained expert, successful traders, and never have exposed ourselves as unprincipled usurpers. But, before Lord Clive urged those restrictive sentiments, they were no longer apposite: the pacific mask was thrown aside, and we stood confessed an insidious, warlike and ambitious race. From that moment the name of Englishman impressed the mind of every Indian power with jealousy and apprehension. Our subsequent misconduct and disasters would already have disarmed their resentments, if they could be pacified with less than our destruction. Till of late they hated, but they dreaded and respected us. To judge by our conduct, the *oderint dum metuant* was our favourite motto; but now they have mingled hatred with contempt. We gained an empire by violence and injustice, it is true; but we maintained

tained it by courage and exploit. We eſtabliſhed over the Aſiatics an aſcendency founded on ſuperior energy and ſkill in every mental and bodily exertion.

Whether it be for the intereſt of England, every circumſtance conſidered, to retain her Indian poſſeſſions, is a queſtion too intricate and important for me to determine; but it appears an irrefragable truth, that if we are to exiſt at all in India, it muſt be in the character of a great, warlike and territorial power——a power at all times able to exalt our allies, and to depreſs our enemies. We may farther venture to aſſert, that if any other ſyſtem be adopted, it will in fact prove an abſolute ſurrender of that country.

The means by which it is yet conceived practicable to reform our civil and military eſtabliſhments having been expreſſed at large in my annexed correſpondence with the Board,

Board, it is unneceſſary to enumerate them at preſent: one thing however is indiſputable, that if Government hope to preſerve a ſhred of their Indian empire, not a moment muſt be loſt in correcting the alarming outrages under which it labours;—in removing thoſe cauſes of diſſention that threaten its exiſtence;—in reforming thoſe abuſes, civil and military, by which its ſtrength has been waſted, and its power decayed; and in bringing every man, meaſure, and reſource, of thoſe diſtracted ſettlements, into one decided point of obedience, co-operation, and effect.

Could we flatter ourſelves, that there is yet vigour, union, and integrity enough in the nation, to atchieve ſuch a re-eſtabliſhment, it would not be chimerical to indulge the moſt exalted expectations.—The intrinſic value of thoſe poſſeſſions would then be fully known to us. We ſhould then recogniſe the ineſtimable benefits, of which an equitable and united Government could render them produc-

 tive

tive beyond all aggregate reſources in the Britiſh empire. The countries ſubject to our influence under any adminiſtration that did not openly cheriſh diſcord, and exult in malverſation, would yield an annual revenue of 10,000,000*l.* ſterling, and would increaſe in value with every ſubſequent improvement. The manufactures of thoſe countries, if at all encouraged, would afford employment for the whole commercial ſtock of England. The ſhipping* engaged in that trade would ſwell into a formidable arma-

* At preſent the India ſhips are mere trading veſſels, without force, diſcipline, or defence; and in time of war are in danger of falling a prey to every well-armed privateer. But the ſlighteſt obſervation muſt ſuggeſt, that they ought to be all conſtructed on the principle of two-deckers, as the Dutch India ſhips are; and, improving on that model, that they ſhould be well armed, completely manned, and ſubject to naval officers under the articles of war. In that event, whenever they had their war complements and inſtructions on board, they would form a fleet ſuperior to any probable attack. If it ſhould ever be judged expedient to build ſhips of force in India, a whole navy might be conſtructed at Bombay, and at other places on the Malabar coaſt, where Teek timber abounds.

ment

ment for the national defence. The resources or finance of those establishments, where 1000*l.* can hardly be raised at this moment, might be fixed on so secure a basis as to support a pile of public credit, more wonderful than that of London or of Amsterdam, and enriched by a circulation more extensive than the whole exchange of Europe.

To crown the series; were it possible for us ever to be consistent, ever to be upright, ever to be trusted, or ever to be trust-worthy in the East; I may venture to assert, that the idea suggested in my annexed letter to the Board, of granting permanent support to the Gentoo interest throughout the Peninsula, in opposition to their invaders and oppressors, would unalterably attach the great mass of the inhabitants to our cause, and leaving their native Rajahs in the full interior direction of their districts, would afford us a volun-

tary

tary contribution more than ſufficient to defray the whole ordinary and contingent charges of our Indian eſtabliſhments. An efficient re-eſpouſal of the cauſe and intereſts of the great Mogul, and of the Muſſulmen who predominate north of the Peninſula, is by no means incompatible with that ſyſtem, and in the preſent ſtate of the northern countries, would render us the immediate Paramounts of Indoſtan.

Thus, my Lord, I have preſumed to lay before you a ſort of Moſaic tablet of our paſt proceedings and preſent ſtate in India. The component parts are not fitted and diſpoſed with the ſkill and ingenuity of a profeſſed artiſt; they are only paſſing ſketches, whoſe utmoſt effect will be produced, if they exhibit to your nice diſcernment, any juſtneſs of perſpective or accuracy of delineation. In the whole courſe of my obſervations I have endeavoured to repreſent men and things in their true proportions, and to place them in their relative positions. Having freely expreſſed my ſentiments on points of ſuch importance to the Britiſh Empire, I ſhould not take the liberty of ſubmitting them to your Lordſhip's inſpection, were I not perſuaded that they convey a faithful portraiture of the ſubject in its real aſpect; and that they tend to confute the fallacies of ſome former productions, which ſeem pencilled by a biaſſed hand, to miſlead the national judgment, and deceive the public eye.

With every ſentiment of attachment and reſpect, I have the honour to be, &c.

LETTER II.*

To Lord MACARTNEY *and the* SELECT COMMITTEE *of Fort St.* GEORGE.

MY LORD, AND GENTLEMEN,

BEFORE I embark for Europe, allow me to exprefs my beft acknowledgements for the approbation with which you have diftinguifhed me, fince I have had the

* This Letter was begun in India, and it was my wifh to have delivered it as a fort of *compte rendu* to the Board of Madras, before my departure from that country. Having been prevented however by unavoidable bufinefs and fevere illnefs, from fulfilling my intention, I left a copy of it at the Cape of Good Hope, to be forwarded from thence to Fort St. George; but that copy had not reached Madras

the honour to command the troops and garrisons south of the Coleroon.—Permit me farther to obtrude on your Lordship and the Board, a brief relation of my proceedings in the command of the southern forces, and of other incidents material to the welfare of your southern territories. Independently of an impulse to state the particulars of my conduct while entrusted with a public charge, I cannot think of leaving India, without presenting to you in one view the merits of the southern army the difficulties under which it laboured, and the services it has performed.—I flatter

Madras when Lord Macartney failed from thence. Since that time I have made many alterations and additions, still preserving the form of address in which the Letter was originally written. This circumstance has betrayed me into several violations of official propriety, in explaining to the Board various incidents and local particulars, with which they were previously acquainted; but without a detail of this nature, the work could hardly have been rendered intelligible to the generality of European readers. In its present form, a copy has been sent to the Court of Directors, that it may be forwarded to Fort St. George, in order to be entered on the records of that presidency.

ter myſelf alſo, that the circumſtances in which I acted, enable me to form an unbiaſſed ſtatement of reſources as they exiſt in thoſe ſouthern countries, of embarraſſments as they have been felt, and of tranſactions as they have been conducted; affording at the ſame time, well-grounded hopes, that, by ſpeedy meaſures of reform, what is beneficial may be improved, and what is amiſs may be corrected *.

To introduce more diſtinctly the narrative of military proceedings that occurred during my command †, it may be neceſſary to ſolicit your attention to a detail of the misfortunes

* The efforts made by Lord Macartney's government to reſtore the ſafety of the Southern Countries, were exemplary and ſucceſsful; but the confuſion in which the war and other circumſtances had involved thoſe territories, rendered it impracticable to carry into immediate execution a complete and general ſyſtem of reform.

† I proceeded to the Southward in October 1782, in the command of the King's troops on that ſtation; and in May 1783 was appointed to ſucceed Colonel Lang, in the general command of the forces ſouth of the river Coleroon.

tunes which previouſly to your Preſident's arrival in India had almoſt entirely exhauſted the reſources and ruined the inhabitants of every diſtrict ſouth of the Coleroon.—Your poſſeſſions in that quarter are of ſufficient magnitude and value to call forth the moſt vigorous endeavours for their protection; but ſuch was their condition when you aſſumed the government, that, without your opportune attentions, they muſt inevitably have been ſevered from the Engliſh dominions.

Thoſe territories, in my opinion, had not obtained their due ſhare of eſtimation under any former Government: divided into various diſtricts, held by different tenures, and occupied by tribes at variance with each other, many parts of them remained uncultivated, and almoſt unexplored. Nor was it practicable for the moſt enlightened of your ſervants, to form a juſt appretiation of the benefits they afford,

afford, until, by the aſſignment of the Nabob of Arcot's revenues to the Company, you were inveſted with the internal management of thoſe countries *.

From the river Coleroon, their northern boundary, which divides them from the Nabobſhip of Arcot, to Cape Comorin, the ſouthern extremity of the Peninſula, is not leſs than 300 miles; and from the ſea which forms their limits on the eaſt, to the countries of Caroor and Dindigul, belonging to Tippoo Sultaun, and the Rajahſhip of Travancore, upon the weſt, is on an average at leaſt 150 miles. Immemorial miſmanagement, and late diſaſter, have hitherto rendered thoſe countries unproductive; but under a ſyſtem in any

* The aſſignment was concluded in the end of the year 1781, between Mahomed Ally and Lord Macartney's government. Previouſly to that arrangement, the Company's ſervants were not allowed to interfere in the territorial affairs of the Nabob.

degree permanent, and founded on the equitable principles that have hitherto directed the conduct of your Lordship and the Board, they would undoubtedly yield an annual revenue of 1,000,000*l.* sterling.

Of those territories, the Rajahship of Tanjore is the most fertile *;—it is watered by a multiplicity of streams, which by means of embankments and reservoirs, are diverted into every field;—it annually affords two or three luxuriant crops of rice;—the forests abound with valuable trees;—the country is overstocked with sheep and cattle;—and formerly teemed with an industrious race, who were expert in agriculture, and habituated to manufacture:—while such are the natural benefits it enjoys, that no spot upon the globe is superior in productions for the use of man.

* The following geographical remarks, which have been inserted since the Letter was originally written, would have been superfluous, if meant only for the Board.

You

You are well apprized, however, that from the establishment of the reigning family of the Maratta race in 1765* to the present period, there has been such a progressive diminution of cultivation, that the annual produce of late years is less by fifty per cent. than it was a century ago.—As Europeans never interfered in the management of that country, and as it has been seldom ravaged or invaded, its decline must be attributed to the malversation of its Maratta or Gentoo administration: but even in its impoverished state †, it used to produce, before the late war, about seventy-five lacks of cullums of rice, worth about eleven lacks of pagodas, or 440,000*l.* sterling:—of this, 160,000*l.* was paid as tribute for your protection, agreeably to the stipulation of 1776, after the last siege

* The country of Tanjore contained 5753 towns and villages at the time when the Maratta government was established.

† See the annual statement of Tanjore produce, in the Appendix.

of

of Tanjore, when the Rajah became a tributary of the Company.—The difficulties that occurred in reducing that capital, the ſtrength of the works, and obſtinacy of the defenders, evince its importance in a military view *:—neither do the inferior forts, and the rivers, rice fields and embankments that interſect the country, afford leſs eminent advantages in the moment of invaſion.

The ſtate of Tritchinopoly, extending from the weſtern limits of Tanjore along the Coleroon, which divides it from the Carnatic on the north, till it reaches Tippoo's dominions on the weſt, near Caroor and Dindigul, including a range of fifty miles by forty, is circumſcribed on the ſouth by the country of Tondiman, and by the woods of Nattam inhabited by Col-

* Tanjore was ſuppoſed to contain 100,000 inhabitants previouſly to the deſtruction that followed Hyder's irruption.

leries.

leries.—Though less valuable than the country of Tanjore, the vicinity of the Coleroon still renders it extremely productive of rice. Under the Nabob Mahomed Ally's management, the expences of collection absorbed the greater part of the revenue arising from this territory, which is at present let to a renter under the assignment of the Nabob's revenues to the Company for about ten lacks of rupees, or 100,000*l.* In prosperous times, however, it possesses the means of extended cultivation, and consequent increase of revenue. The size and situation of the city, the abundance of subsistence in the district, and the long residence of the Nabob Mahomed Ally's second son the Ameer Ul Omrah at that place, have rendered it the favourite establishment of the Mussulmen to the southward of the Coleroon. The two great Pagodas of Jumbakistna and Seringham, on the adjacent island of Seringham, command the veneration of Gentoos; while every spot on that

 island

island on the opposite or northern side of the Coleroon, about Semiaveram and Volkondah, as well as on the plains of Tritchinopoly, are recorded for the bloody contests of Chunda Saheb, Astruc, Clive, and Lawrence; and mark with classical reverence the scene of those atchievements. But above all, it becomes important in a political and military view, as the strongest and most advanced garrison upon your frontiers towards the territories of Mysore, and the best position for cantoning your army, in order to menace that power *.

The country of the Colleries, including the territories of Tondiman, Mellore, and Nattam, extends from the sea-coast to the confines of Madura in a range of sixty miles by sixty-five †. With the exception of some

* See my Letter to the Board, dated the 26th of April 1784.

† Tondiman is less uncultivated than his neighbours, and has at all times proved himself the most faithful adherent

ſome ſpots which have accidentally been cultivated, it is overgrown with thickets, and inhabited by ſavage tribes. Before that country can be rendered valuable, the woods muſt be cleared, the ſtrong holds occupied, and the Colleries compelled to relinquiſh their predatory habits: for, in its preſent condition, fertile tracts are loſt to cultivation, and the wild inhabitants, amounting to 30 or 40,000 men in arms under different Chiefs, are ever ready to increaſe the public danger in the moments of hoſtility.

The territory of Shevigunga, or the Little Marawa, ſtretches from the ſea-coaſt on the eaſt, to the diſtricts of Mellore and Madura on the weſt, and from the country of Tondiman and the Nattam Colleries

herent of the Nabob and of the Company. The father of the preſent Chief, by his firmneſs and attachment, in the days of General Lawrence, ſupplied the force at Tritchinopoly with proviſions, at a time when their cauſe ſeemed deſperate. And the Nabob, ſenſible of the obligation, ever afterwards exempted him from tribute.

the north, to the territories of the Great Marawa on the south; containing about fifty miles in length and forty in breadth. The soil in general is unfriendly to the growth of corn, though not quite destitute of running streams or artificial reservoirs; but the country is overgrown with thorns and bushes. The woods of Calicoil extend nearly forty miles in circumference. They are secured with barriers, and other defences around the fort of Calicoil, which is situated in the centre of the thickets, and considered as a refuge from exaction or invasion. These woods, and the surrounding country, abound with sheep and cattle: — the inhabitants are numerous, and can bring 12,000 fighting men into the field, armed with swords, pikes, spears, and firelocks. Though less barbarous than the Colleries their neighbours, yet arts and industry have made little progress among them. The

country

fome fpots which have accidentally been cultivated, it is overgrown with thickets, and inhabited by favage tribes. Before that country can be rendered valuable, the woods muft be cleared, the ftrong holds occupied, and the Colleries compelled to relinquifh their predatory habits: for, in its prefent condition, fertile tracts are loft to cultivation, and the wild inhabitants, amounting to 30 or 40,000 men in arms under different Chiefs, are ever ready to increafe the public danger in the moments of hoftility.

The territory of Shevigunga, or the Little Marawa, ftretches from the fea-coaft on the eaft, to the diftricts of Mellore and Madura on the weft, and from the country of Tondiman and the Nattam Colleries

herent of the Nabob and of the Company. The father of the prefent Chief, by his firmnefs and attachment, in the days of General Lawrence, fupplied the force at Tritchinopoly with provifions, at a time when their caufe feemed defperate. And the Nabob, fenfible of the obligation, ever afterwards exempted him from tribute.

 upon

upon the north, to the territories of the Great Marawa on the ſouth; containing about fifty miles in length and forty in breadth. The ſoil in general is unfriendly to the growth of corn, though not quite deſtitute of running ſtreams or artificial reſervoirs; but the country is overgrown with thorns and buſhes. The woods of Calicoil extend nearly forty miles in circumference. They are ſecured with barriers, and other defences around the fort of Calicoil, which is ſituated in the centre of the thickets, and conſidered as a refuge from exaction or invaſion. Theſe woods, and the ſurrounding country, abound with ſheep and cattle:—the inhabitants are numerous, and can bring 12,000 fighting men into the field, armed with ſwords, pikes, ſpears, and firelocks. Though leſs barbarous than the Colleries their neighbours, yet arts and induſtry have made little progreſs among them. The

country

the Nabob is one lack and 75,000 rupees. The reduction of the country in the year 1773 by General Joseph Smith, and a garrison of the Nabob's troops constantly stationed in the capital, have deprived the native prince even of personal freedom. Still however he is venerated by Gentoos, on account of his high descent, and as the guardian of the sacred waters and Pagoda of Ramiserum.

I come now to the state of Madura, bounded by Mellore on the east, by the Nattam Colleries on the north, by the country of Dindigul, belonging to Hyder, on the west, and by Tinivelly on the south. Its territory is not more than forty-five miles in length and thirty-five in breadth, and its annual revenue is diminished to 34,000*l.* When the Gentoo Rajah Trimalnaigue reigned there in the last century, his territories extended over many parts of the southern countries. His treasures were great,

great, and the monuments of magnificence left by him, which are hardly ſurpaſſed in any age or country, ſtill remain a melancholy contraſt with preſent poverty and depopulation. The gallant reſiſtance made by Mahomed Iſſoof, when he diſclaimed allegiance to the Nabob Mahomed Ally, is a ſufficient proof that when the works are in repair, this place may be defended againſt the moſt powerful Indian enemy; while its vicinity to the country of Dindigul, belonging to Tippoo Sultaun, renders it a poſition of capital importance in the event of any future operations againſt that power.

The laſt but not the leaſt conſiderable of your ſouthern territories is Tinivelly, which is divided by a ridge of inacceſſible mountains on the north from the wild valleys of Watrap and Outumpollam belonging to Tippoo Sultaun. It ſtretches to the confines of Madura and Ramnad on the northeaſt and eaſt, reaches to the ſea upon the ſouth, and borders on the weſt with the Rajahſhip of Travancore, both terminating near Cape Comorin. Its ſurface is generally flat from the ſea coaſt, till it approaches the mountains on its northern boundary. Nature has been peculiarly bountiful to this province:—The rivers by which it is interſected, enſure luxuriant crops of rice, and the drieſt parts yield cotton in abundance. The productions that enrich the neighbouring iſland of Ceylon would flouriſh here, and might render us the rivals of the Dutch in the cinnamon trade: but the particular tenure under which Tinivelly has been held, the convulſions it has endured from the firſt intruſions of the Muſſulmen in the courſe of this century, and the depravity of its rulers, have counteracted the benefits of nature. Even when a native Rajah governed this province, the flat and open country only was reduced, and was let for ſpecific ſums to great renters, who were inveſted with

with despotic powers, and harassed the peaceful subject; while various leaders, possessing considerable territory, maintained armed force, and withheld their stipulated tribute on the first appearance of disturbance. These chiefs, who at present amount in number to thirty-two, are capable of bringing 30,000 brave though undisciplined troops into the field; they have also fortified towns and strong-holds in the mountains, whither they retire in cases of emergency.

Beside the territory that these chiefs, who as well as their subjects are called Polygars, possess under the range of hills that forms the northern boundary of Tinivelly, many of them hold ample tracks in the flat and cultivated country. Adverse to industry, they suffer their own possessions to remain waste, while they invade each other, and plunder their industrious neighbours. Such is the dread of those ravagers, that every district

diſtrict in the province has been forced to purchaſe their forbearance by enormous contributions. In this ſituation, you have rather cauſe to wonder that your ſuperintendant, Mr. Irwin, ſhould have been enabled to procure ſo large an increaſe of revenue, than that the produce of this country ſhould in no recorded period have born any proportion to its natural advantages.

The preceding obſervations can only be conſidered as a haſty outline of the Company's poſſeſſions ſouth of the Coleroon; which, in extent, are nearly equal to the Carnatic; but in point of ſoil, water, ſituation, and capability of improvement, ſurpaſs any diſtrict under your control.

The calamities with which the invaſion of Hyder Ally in 1781 overwhelmed the Carnatic, fell heavily upon the ſouthern countries. No ſooner had the multitudes under

under that ravager poured down from the mountains of Myſore, than deſolation extended acroſs the Coleroon. Thouſands of his plunderers overran the countries of Kivelore, Tanjore, Tritchinopoly, and Madura. A moſt luxuriant crop, with which the ground was at that time covered, was inſtantly ſwept off, and every water-dyke and embankment totally deſtroyed. The inhabitants who eſcaped the ſword, ſought ſhelter in the forts; where, adding miſery to diſtreſs, they periſhed in the ſtreets; while the whole country, laid waſte by fire and ſword, exhibited the ſad reality of a general conflagration. At length Hyder, having left nothing to deſtroy in the Carnatic, and regardleſs of our force, which from the time of Colonel Baillie's defeat had never ventured from its encampment near Madras, reſolved to lead in perſon his victorious army to the ſouthward. After remaining ſome weeks encamped within random ſhot of Tanjore,

Tanjore, he proceeded to invest Tritchinopoly, and threatened to fill up the ditch with his Moormen's slippers. The repeated checks sustained by the Company's troops in that quarter, the corps that Hyder had cut off, and the forts he had reduced, spread so general a consternation, that the important and defenceless garrison of Tritchinopoly seemed ready to surrender. In that event the southern countries must have submitted to his power, had not the repulse of Sir Eyre Coote's army against Chilumbrum elated Hyder with the hopes of defeating the only force that could endanger his conquest. This induced him to renounce more solid, though less brilliant prospects, and to fight the battle of the 1st July 1781 at Porto Novo.

Notwithstanding his ill success in that engagement, and his personal absence from the southward, our affairs in that quarter still remained in great confusion. The Tanjore country was occupied by the enemy, who ſecured its crops and cattle, repulſed the Company's troops at Tricatapooly, Putticottah, and Trivelore, and confined them within the fort of Tanjore. There, the granaries were empty, the Rajah's ſubjects diſaffected, and he himſelf accuſed of negotiating with Hyder, and of introducing arms clandeſtinely into his palace. He likewiſe ſuffered the whole crops of his country to be collected by the enemy, while he reſiſted every ſolicitation to fill his magazines, and provide for impending events.

The defeat of Colonel Braithwaite in February 1782, and the loſs of his detachment (attacked by a powerful army under Tippoo Sultaun), would have proved a deadly blow, had it not been warded off by the active abilities and conciliating manners of Mr. Sulivan, to whom the ſafety of Tanjore and of all the ſouthern provinces was then

then juſtly aſcribed. The ſubſequent capture of Colonel Horne, proceeding to the ſouthward from the Preſidency with military ſupplies, added extremely to the diſtreſs and embarraſſment experienced at Tanjore. In the provinces ſouth of Tanjore and Tritchinopoly, the proſpect was not leſs alarming. The Great Marawa country was infeſted by a hoſt of rebels under Maupely Taver, a relation of the reigning family, who over-ran the territory, occupied its beſt poſitions, and for many months inveſted the garriſon of Ramnad.

The Little Marawa country was controlled by Perry and China Mordeen, who after the murder of the late Rajah in 1773, had fled to the protection of Hyder, and returning at the time of his invaſion, maintained the country under his authority, keeping the infant Rajah a ſtate-priſoner, and ravaging the territories of the Company and Nabob.

The diſtricts of Madura, Mellore, and Palemery, were ſo haraſſed with Colleries, Polygars, and the enemy, that your troops and ſubjects were often attacked within range of the forts, and the ſentries fired at on the works. All the Polygars of Tinivelly were in rebellion, and cloſely connected with the Dutch government at Colombo, from whence attempts were meditated, in conjunction with them and with Maupely Taver, to reduce thoſe countries and the Marawa dominions. Near 100,000 Polygars and Colleries were in arms throughout the ſouthern provinces, and, being hoſtile to Government, conſidered public confuſion as the only ſafeguard againſt puniſhment. To repreſs theſe outrages, and to retrieve your affairs in the preſent exigency, your ſouthern force was inadequate. The treaſury was drained,—the country depopulated,—the revenues exacted by the enemy,—and the troops undiſciplined,

ciplined, poorly fed, and unſucceſsfully commanded *.

The complicated dangers ariſing from this ſituation of the country induced you, in September 1782, to ſend a reinforcement of Europeans and Artillery to the Southward, under the command of Colonel Lang. You were led to hope that this detachment, when reinforced by the troops to be collected from every quarter of the South, might have materially promoted the views of Colonel Humberſtone, who was then at Paniani, preparing to proceed againſt Palacatcherry, and to penetrate into Coimbatour, according to the plan ſuggeſted by Mr. Sulivan, approved of by your Lordſhip and the Board, and afterwards carried into

* Such was the ſtate of affairs to the Southward when Lord Macartney's Government commenced, and for ſome time afterwards authority in military matters was veſted in Sir Eyre Coote by the Supreme Board; but as ſoon as that authority was reſtored to the Governor and Select Committee, they made the moſt meritorious efforts to provide for the ſafety of the ſouthern countries.

 execution

execution by myself. But from a variety of circumstances it happened, that the operations of Colonel Lang were confined to the reduction of Caroor, Aravarcourchy, and Dindigul. Being limited in his movements to those districts of the enemy, and to the track between Negapatam, Tanjore, and Tritchinopoly, the southern countries continued nearly in their former state of desolation. Many as the representations were that reached your Board on this subject, it would have been desirable for you in person to have beheld the malversations that had been committed, the miseries that were endured, and the patience of your subjects under unsupportable grievances.

The ravages of the enemy, however, were by no means the greatest evils that those districts had sustained. There were inherent and increasing causes of decline: cultivation was neglected,—the husbandmen were killed or driven off,—the cattle were

were wild,—and the fields were desolate. Yet over this wilderness, the Renter, the Amuldar, the Monagar, the Tesseldar, and all the instruments of public exaction, tyrannised with unabating rigour. The forts, excepting Tanjore, were neglected and decaying;—the military stores had been in a great measure expended or embezzled; and those that now remained were ill constructed and worse arranged;—the military Storekeepers, Grainkeepers, Paymasters and Commissaries, belonging to the civil service, were habituated to disavow any controlling power in the Commandant of the place;—nor were the exhortations and example of Mr. Sulivan sufficient to correct the evil. Hence disorder arose in those departments. The civil and military, the King and Company's officers, were at variance. The adherents of the Nabob were loud in their complaints against Europeans, while the Tanjorines extended their aversion to all classes of our countrymen. The large arrears due to the

 troops,

troops, and other grievances, rendered it impracticable for officers to maintain strict discipline in their corps; as it required the utmost efforts to prevent mutiny among men, who, brave and faithful as they undoubtedly were, could hardly be blamed for clamour and complaint when reduced to procure subsistence by selling their own children!

The discordant powers of the civil servants in the different departments increased the evils already enumerated. Such was the extent of those evils, that the ablest persons at one time despaired of retrieving your affairs in that quarter; nor was it held practicable to maintain the southern army in the field, dispirited by defeat, and destitute of resources*.

* No circumstance could tend more clearly to evince the meritorious efforts of Lord Macartney, than his having been able to retrieve the southern provinces from the wretched condition to which he found them reduced on his accession to the Government.

Some

Some preceding incidents, however, proved the inefficiency of that defenſive ſyſtem under which the Carnatic war had been conducted, indicated offenſive operation, as the only means of future proſperity, and confirmed the merit of thoſe endeavours made by your Lordſhip and the Board to attack the enemy in his own poſſeſſions*. On this principle Colonel Humberſtone had acted on the Malabar coaſt. He obliged Tippoo Saib to march acroſs the peninſula, and to retire with loſs from

* Lord Macartney's ſyſtem of promoting offenſive operations againſt Tippoo Sultaun does him peculiar honour; not only on account of the judgment that ſuggeſted theſe ideas, and the vigour with which they were carried into execution in moments of great difficulty, and againſt the opinions of powerful opponents, but alſo from the eminent ſucceſs with which they were attended. Beſides directing the ſouthern army to penetrate into the richeſt poſſeſſions of Tippoo Sultaun, his Lordſhip reinforced the Malabar army under Colonels Macleod and Humberſtone, and formed a conſiderable force in the Northern Circars, under General Jones; thus diſtracting the enemy's attention, and enabling the Engliſh arms to regain their aſcendency.

the

the engagement in November 1782 at Paniani *. The subsequent success of General Matthews against Mangalore, Beddanore, and the principal forts of the adjacent countries, still farther evinced the wisdom of Mr. Sulivan's opinions, and of Colonel Humberstone's operations. Tippoo was forced to march from Arcot to Beddanore; his father's death in December 1782 having made him cross the peninsula from Paniani to Arcot. This event relieved the Carnatic, and was the first circumstance during the war that gave a turn to our affairs. For the movements and counter-movements of the Carnatic army, and even the repeated defeats sustained by Hyder, had proved of little ultimate avail in the decision of the contest.

* It is impossible for me to do justice to Colonel Humberstone as a man and as an officer. A narrative of the services he performed in command of the forces on the Malabar coast, would afford convincing proof of his distinguished military talents, and add to the regret which his untimely loss occasioned in the minds of all who knew his merits and his character.

At

At this crisis it was fortunate for the English interests, that your Lordship and the Board resolved to direct the southern troops to make every effort against the enemy. The first object of my command was to augment our field force, by battalions from Tanjore, Tritchinopoly, and Tinivelly. The zealous support of Mr. Sulivan and Mr. Irwin speedily enabled me to equip the army, and to prosecute offensive operations; which your Lordship and the Board judged to be essential to the re-establishment of the public welfare.

The high sense I entertained of the treaty formed by Mr. Sulivan under your Government, for the restoration of the ancient Gentoo family of Mysore, formerly deposed, and still confined by Hyder, was only equalled by my attachment to the system of conciliating all classes of the natives. This was no less congenial with the general tenor of your conduct, than with

with the ſpirit of Mr. Sulivan's negotiations, and was requiſite to give effect to his enlightened views. In ſupport of theſe ideas, the abilities as well as influence of the Bramins rendered it eſſential to treat them with particular indulgence; and by ſimilar attentions the numerous Polygars of Dindigul were reconciled to our intereſts, as has been fully evinced by the ſupplies derived from thoſe poſſeſſions while under our Government.

The dependents of his highneſs the Nabob* felt themſelves extremely humbled by the aſſignment of his territory to the Company. For however eligible and indiſpenſable this meaſure might appear on principles of public neceſſity, it could not fail to deprive his adherents of their power and ſituation. As far as depended

* As the dependents of the Nabob are in general Mahometans, this obſervation does not apply to the Gentoos, who form the great body of inhabitants in the Nabob's country.

upon

upon me I endeavoured to convince them all, that their wants ſhould be relieved, their rights protected, and their conſequence maintained. They were pleaſed to credit my declarations, and by theſe means we reſtrained the diſſatisfaction of the inhabitants and native ſoldiery, many of whom are warmly attached to the Nabob, and were ready to burſt forth in the moſt alarming diſorders. The ſame principle formed the rule of my conduct towards the Rajah of Tanjore and the other chiefs whoſe countries fell within the limits of my command—conſcious, that all our meaſures reſpecting the native Princes and their ſubjects, ſhould be directed by liberal conceſſion and unbiaſſed juſtice.

My next endeavour was, in conjunction with Mr. Sulivan, to unite all deſcriptions of men in cordial exertions to retrieve the public intereſts, and to enure the troops to diſcipline and enterpriſe; without which they

they neither could be ſubſiſted, nor could we hope for any reputable termination of our ill-fated conteſt. That theſe attempts have not proved entirely unproductive of important public benefits, has been repeatedly teſtified by your Board in terms moſt flattering to myſelf.

By the 25th of May, the army marched from Dindigul towards Daraporam, which fell to us on the 2d of June*. That valuable place affords ample ſupplies of grain

* The particulars of the attack and ſurrender of this place are expreſſed in my Letter of the 2d of June, addreſſed to the Governor and Select Committee. One circumſtance deſerves to be mentioned, in order to prove the ingenuity of intelligencers in India. When the army encamped before Daraporam, it was not practicable to approach ſo near the fort as to determine with preciſion the moſt advantageous point of attack; but a Braman Harcarrah explained every particular reſpecting the poſition of the works, and the nature of the ground adjoining to the place, in ſuch terms as enabled me to draw a plan from his deſcription. The Adjutant General Captain Oram did the ſame, from the accounts of another intelligencer. On comparing the two plans, thus drawn from verbal informa-

grain and cattle, is capable of considerable defence, and is far advanced in the enemy's country, being equally distant from the two coasts. Although the position of an army there would always be of eminent advantage, it was more peculiarly so when we reduced it, because Tippoo Sultaun had recovered Beddanore, captured General Matthews, and invested Mangalore. The southern army was not in sufficient strength to think of marching to Seringapatam*, and was so far from being able to oppose the whole power of Tippoo Sultaun, that we could not even afford to garrison Daraporam, and were obliged to destroy the fortification. Yet we might assuredly have reduced the rich tract that lies below the

information, we found such topographical resemblance that we marched a body of troops in a dark night, crossed a river, and occupied a strong position within 400 yards of the fort, from whence we erected our batteries and effected a breach.

* The capital of Mysore.

moun-

mountains of Myſore*, which would probably have forced Tippoo Sultaun to raiſe the ſiege of Mangalore, and march his main body againſt us; or if Tippoo had perſiſted againſt Mangalore, we ſhould have amply ſubſiſted the army, have reduced a valuable territory, and prepared for more important conqueſts.

General Stuart's order on the 31ſt of May, to march towards him at Cuddelore with the utmoſt expedition, obliged me to relinquiſh thoſe advantages. You were pleaſed to think favourably of my precautions for the defence of Dindigul, which was garriſoned with the ſixth Car-

* Extending from Caroor to Combatour, and from the bottom of the hills to the confines of Madura and Tritchinopoly. A country abounding in every kind of production for the ſupport of armies, and which may be conſidered as a chain of magazines eſtabliſhed by Tippoo Sultaun for the invaſion of the Southern Provinces, in the ſame manner as the Burmaul country may be conſidered as affording him the means of invaſion on the eaſt.

natic

natic battalion, and a body of the Nabob's independents*. Some heavy guns and military ſtores were likewiſe thrown into the place, and directions given that grain might be collected, wood prepared, and every effort made to enſure a deſperate reſiſtance. The fort of Aravarcourchy † had been deſtroyed ſoon after its reduction; and, in obedience to your orders reſpecting the demolition of Caroor ‡, mines were conſtructed, and the works blown up. My inſtructions to the ſouthern commandants reſpecting the diſtribution of their troops, and preparations for defence, likewiſe received your commendation.

* Dindigul is ſituated in a rich valley of the ſame name, about fifty miles ſouth-weſt from Caroor. The town is large, and well fortified; its principal ſtrength conſiſts in a very high and almoſt inacceſſible rock, on which there is a fortreſs that might be rendered impregnable: but the ſouthern army took the place by ſtorm in May 1783.

† Aravarcourchy was taken by aſſault in April 1783. About 500 people were killed in the attack.

‡ Caroor is a place of very conſiderable ſtrength, fifty miles from Tritchinopoly, on the frontiers of the Myſore dominions; was reduced by the ſouthern army in April 1783, after ſeveral weeks of open trenches, and contained great quantities of proviſions, ſtores, and ammunition.

On our arrival at Tritchinopoly in June, the troops were ſupplied with grain, the gun-carriages repaired, cattle collected for the army at Cuddelore, and boats provided for croſſing the Cavery and Coleroon, which with two intermediate ſtreams were then unfordable. At Munſurpet on the northern bank of the Coleroon, I received farther inſtructions from General Stuart to march without delay to Cuddelore. The injunctions of your Board no leſs pointedly directed me to recroſs the river, and continue to the ſouthward. But you had been pleaſed to inveſt me with a diſcretional latitude of acting as exigencies might require; and intelligence had reached me that Suffrein's ſquadron had anchored at Cuddelore, that a diſembarkation of many thouſand men was intended, and that the Engliſh army was haraſſed with the duty of the trenches. It appeared therefore to be moſt congenial with the general tenor of your intentions, that we ſhould march towards General Stuart, being conſcious that the public ſafety could have no exiſtence if his army were defeated. Colonel Forbes, who remained in command of the ſouthern provinces, inſpired every one around him with a full reliance on his zeal and military talents; and I ſhall ever gratefully acknowledge, that on the firſt communication of thoſe proceedings, you were pleaſed to honour me with your approbation.

Upon our arrival within three forced marches of General Stuart's camp, a ceſſation of hoſtility with the French was announced, and we returned towards the ſouthward*. The ſame diſpatches intimated General Stuart's ſuſpenſion, and that General Bruce commanded the Carnatic army. I wrote to General Bruce, offering to make an unexpected movement againſt the fort of Salem, which ſecures the moſt important paſs from the Carnatic into Myſore, and contained many months proviſions for an army; adding, that nothing would be requiſite on

* July 1783.

 the

the part of General Bruce, but to ſend a force ſufficient to garriſon the place, until he could move thither with the troops from Cuddelore. The General finding it neceſſary to reject this propoſal, we left him to ſtruggle with his difficulties, and proceeded to Munſurpet.

My intention was to move next day by Tarriore to reinſtate your tributary the Rheddey in his paternal inheritance, and to advance againſt the forts and magazines of Settimungulum, Namcul, and Sankerry-durgum on the north of the Coleroon; from thence to croſs the river and beſiege Erode, with a view of eſtabliſhing a ſtrong garriſon at that place, and in order to prepare ſupplies for moving, when ſufficiently reinforced, againſt Seringapatam. But our expectations were diſappointed by your intimations of an armiſtice with Tippoo Sultaun.

During the courſe of theſe proceedings, it was found impracticable to carry into exe-

execution the ſalutary meaſures intended by your Board, for the re-eſtabliſhment of public authority in your ſouthern provinces, which unavoidably remained in their former confuſion. The Polygars, Colleries, and other tributaries, ever ſince the commencement of the war, had thrown off all appearance of allegiance. No civil arrangement could be attempted without a military force, and nothing leſs than the whole army ſeemed adequate to their reduction. While ſuch a conſiderable portion of the ſouthern provinces remained in defiance of the Company's government, it was vain to think of ſupporting the current charges of the eſtabliſhment; far leſs could we hope to reduce the arrears, and to prepare for important operations, in the probable event of a recommencement of hoſtility. It became indiſpenſable therefore, to reſtore the tranquillity of thoſe provinces by vigorous military meaſures,

 as

as the only means that could render them productive of revenue; and in this view, your wiſe arrangements for augmenting the ſouthern force, proved not leſs beneficial, than in their influence on the operations againſt the enemy.

You had been pleaſed to reinforce us with 500 Europeans and two battalions of Sepoys under Colonel Stuart, immediately after the ſiege of Cuddelore; another detachment of equal ſtrength marched towards us under Colonel Elphinſton. It was my intention to have joined thoſe corps at Dindigul, in order to act againſt Tippoo, in caſe he ſhould not accede to the terms propoſed; but finding that the detachment could not reach Dindigul for many weeks, it appeared eligible to employ the intermediate ſpace in fulfilling the objects already ſtated. In concurrence therefore with the requiſitions of Mr. Sulivan,

Sulivan *, we proceeded to Mellore, in order to awe the rebellious Colleries of that diſtrict. We left a ſtrong body encamped there, and marched with the remaining troops on the 4th of Auguſt to Shevigunga, about twenty miles eaſt from thence. The two Murdeens, who rule the little Marawa, fled precipitately with their young Rajah to the woods of Calicoil, and collected their force to the amount of 10,000 men: nor could they be prevailed on to return to their habitations and truſt to my aſſurances.

Beſides the immediate diſcharge of their arrears of tribute, I demanded from their deputies 90,000 rupees, in compenſation to the Company for the ravages they had committed; and concluded with declaring, that if theſe conditions were not fulfilled, we ſhould attack their woods, ſtorm their

* Reſident of Tanjore, and Superintendant of aſſigned revenues of Tritchinopoly and the Marawas.

fort, and drive them from the country. Notwithſtanding the procraſtinating ſpirit of Gentoos, they paid near 40,000 rupees, and gave ſecurity for their remaining debt.

The lenity and diſpatch of this tranſaction (for it was concluded in four days) afforded a cordial ſatisfaction when contraſted with the circumſtances of the expedition in 1773, againſt this very place. On that occaſion the Rajah, truſting to the woods and barriers that ſurround the fort of Calicoil, and expecting to conclude the buſineſs by negotiation, conceived himſelf in ſecurity when the place was ſurpriſed, and he was killed on the attack. I rejoiced to mitigate the rigorous treatment which the delinquency of the ſucceſſor, or rather of his miniſters, merited, in conſideration of the ſeverities which the predeceſſor had experienced.

There next remained a more important undertaking. The numerous Polygars of Tini-

Tinivelly, who had rebelled on the commencement of the war, committed daily ravages from Madura to Cape Comorin. They subdued forts, and occupied districts belonging to the Circar*, or held by a tenure different from their own. Mr. Irwin, superintendant of Madura and Tinivelly, had repeatedly urged me to proceed against the Polygars, in order to restore tranquillity and recover the revenues. It was now for the first time in my power to direct my operations towards that quarter, at a moment when the most powerful of the Polygars in confederacy against your Government, and in alliance with the Dutch, had assembled 12 or 14,000 men, and were actually besieging the fort of Chocumpetty, a Polygar place of some strength, below the hills that form the north-west boundary of the province.

* Circar means the ruling power of the country, and the detail of its revenue.

When

When it was determined that we should march into Tinivelly, during the interval requisite for Colonels Stuart and Elphinston's detachments to reach Dindigul, my object was to strike an unexpected blow, and to intimidate the Polygars into submission. Of all the Tinivelly chiefs, the principal in power and delinquency, excepting Shevigherry, was Catabominaigue: he was personally engaged at the siege of Chocumpetty, from whence his fort of Pandalamcourchy, on the south-east quarter of Tinivelly, is distant more than seventy miles. The usual route to Tinivelly passes by Madura; and the Polygars, hearing of our movement towards Shevigunga, expected us in that direction. To favour this opinion, provisions for the army were ordered to be prepared at Madura; my real intention was perfectly concealed; and we moved off with the force from Shevigunga, in the evening of the 8th of August, to Tripechetty, a place twenty miles distant on the

the southern border of the Mellore country. We there joined the remainder of the army, and leaving the seventh battalion and some irregulars under Captain Oliver to restrain the Colleries at Mellore, proceeded next morning by Pallemery, Pandalgoody and Naiglapour, and reached the fort of Pandalamcourchy on the fourth day, being 100 miles from Shevigunga*.

As soon as the line approached the fort, a flag was sent, desiring the headmen to open their gates and hold a conference: they refused. The eighteen-pounders were therefore halted in the rear of an embankment facing the north-east angle of the works; a hasty battery was constructed; and in three hours we were ready to open on the bastion. The works were manned with several thousand people, and every circumstance denoted an intention of resistance.

* Fahrenheit's thermometer was frequently above 110 degrees during these marches.

ance. It was material to ſtorm without delay, in order to ſtrike terror by diſpatch, and alſo leſt Catabominaigue with his confederate chiefs might haſten to obſtruct our operations. We opened on the baſtion; but finding ourſelves retarded by its thickneſs, we reſolved to breach the adjoining curtain, and to render the defences of the baſtion untenable by the beſieged. They kept up a conſtant and well-directed fire, and notwithſtanding our utmoſt efforts, it was dark before a practicable breach was effected. The attack was therefore deferred until the moon ſhould riſe. The ſtorming party conſiſted of two companies of Europeans, ſupported by the thirteenth and twenty-fourth Carnatic battalions, and continued in the rear of the battery: the cavalry, the firſt, and light infantry battalions, were poſted at right angles with the other three ſalient angles of the fort, with detachments fronting each gateway, in order to prevent the beſieged from receiving ſupplies, or making

making their escape, while the other troops remained to defend the camp, which was within random-shot.

Our next object was to remove a strong hedge fronting the breach and surrounding the whole fort, as is the practice in the Polygar system of defence. This dangerous service was effected with unusual skill, by Ensign Cunningham, commanding the pioneers; and about ten at night, with the advantage of bright moon-shine, the storm commenced. Our troops, after they gained the summit of the breach, found no sufficient space to lodge themselves; and the interior wall having no slope or talus, they could not push forward from the summit as they advanced. The defenders were numerous, and opposed us so vigorously with pikes and musquetry, that we were obliged at last to retire and reach the battery, with considerable slaughter on both sides. Immediate measures were taken to renew the charge;

charge; but the Polygars, diſpirited with their loſs, abandoned the place, and sallied forth at the eaſtern gate.

The corps poſted round the works were ſo exhauſted by the preceding marches, that many of the fugitives effected their eſcape: the reſt were taken priſoners. The breach was covered with dead bodies, and the place contained a large aſſortment of guns, powder, ſhot, arms, and other military ſtores, which were of courſe applied to the public ſervice: 40,000 pagodas were alſo found, and immediately diſtributed to the troops. Your Board were pleaſed to confirm the diſtribution, on the footing of prize-money; than which no meaſure could more effectually tend to animate the army in our after-operations. Some other facts reſpecting theſe tranſactions, and the treaty between the Dutch Government of Colombo and Catabominaigue (of which the original was taken in his fort), were referred to to in my letters of the 13th of Auguſt, addreſſed to your Lordſhip and the Board*.

Having left Captain Jacobs with five companies of the 25th battalion to garriſon the place, I proceeded to Palamcottah, in order to inſpect the ſtate of that fort; and from thence moved with the army by Shankanakoil to Shevigerry. It was hoped that the reduction of that ſtrong-hold, belonging to the moſt powerful of all the Polygars, in addition to the fall of Pandalamcourchy, would intimidate the leſs conſiderable offenders, and convince the whole confederacy that their treatment would be proportioned to their miſconduct. Beſides, the outrages committed by the Shevigerry Chief were atrocious, and could not be forgiven without a total ſurrender of your authority. He had barbarouſly murdered Captain Graham Campbell, and cut off a detachment

* See the letter of the 13th of Auguſt, inſerted in the Appendix.

under

under command of that officer. On former occasions, he had beat off considerable detachments, and avowedly protected your enemies, who thought themselves secure in the fort of Shevigerry. He had collected magazines sufficient to supply the Dutch force that was expected from Colombo, as well as to resist the most tedious blockade; for he did not conceive his fort could be stormed, and every circumstance in his conduct marked, that he held himself beyond the reach of military power.

On our arrival before the town of Shevigerry he retired to the thickets near four miles deep in front of his Comby*, which it covers and defends. He manned the whole extent of a strong embankment, that separates the wood and open country; was joined by Catabominaigue, with other associated Polygars, and mustered 8 or 9,000 men in arms.

* A strong-hold in the mountains.

In

In the present instance lenity would have been accounted imbecility; but the approach of Colonels Stuart and Elphinston to Dindigul, and Tippoo Sultaun's refusal of the proposed accommodation, rendered me extremely anxious to finish this Polygar warfare, in order to proceed towards the enemy's frontiers. The Shevigerry chief and his associates were therefore informed, that we meant immediately to attack the place, unless they would convene the Head Polygars of Tinivelly, amounting to thirty-two chiefs, liquidate all arrears, and refund the amount of depredations committed since the commencement of the war, agreeably to authenticated vouchers in the different districts. It was farther intimated, that if they, on the part of the confederacy, would engage to pay 120,000*l.* in lieu of all demands, their proposal should be forwarded to the superintendant of revenue (Mr. Irwin), and on his acceptance, that the troops

 would

would be withdrawn, and that they would be recommended to forgiveneſs. They wiſhed to confer with me, but refuſed to viſit me in camp. As their diſtruſt aroſe from various outrages committed againſt them by former commanders, inſtead of increaſing their apprehenſions by reſentment, I propoſed to meet them alone and unattended at their own barrier; adding that if any accident befel me, it would not paſs unreſented. The Shevigerry chief, Catabominaigue, and the depoſed Polygar of Chocumpetty, with a large retinue, met me in front of their embankment. Before they finiſhed their explanations, it was dark, and a muſket inadvertently fired in the rear alarmed our advanced picket, who thought it was aimed at me. To prevent the ill conſequences of that miſtake, I took leave of the Polygars, expreſſing my wiſh to hear of their acceding to the terms propoſed. We refrained from hoſtility next day, but finding that they trifled with our

our proposals, the line was ordered under arms on the morning following, and we made the distribution of attack. It proved as desperate as any contest in that species of Indian warfare; not only from the numbers and obstinacy of the Polygars, but from the peculiar circumstances which had acquired this place the reputation of impregnable.

The attack commenced, by the Europeans and four battalions of Sepoys moving against the embankment which covers the wood. The Polygars in full force opposed us, but our troops remained with their firelocks shouldered under a heavy fire, until they approached the embankment; there they gave a general discharge and rushed upon the enemy. By the vigour of this advance we got possession of the summit, and the Polygars took post on the verge of the adjoining wood, disputing every step with great loss on both sides.

 After

After reconnoitring, we found that the Comby could not be approached in front. We proceeded therefore to cut a road through impenetrable thickets for three miles, to the base of the hill that bounds the Comby on the west. The pioneers under Ensign Cunningham laboured with indefatigable industry; Captain Gardiner of the 102d supported them with the Europeans, and Captain Blacker with the third and twenty-fourth Carnatic battalions, advanced their field-pieces as fast as the road was cleared. These were strengthened by troops in their rear, forming a communication with those in front; for this purpose two other battalions were posted within the wood, and as soon as we gained the embankment, the camp moved near it, and concentrated our force.

We continued to cut our way under an unabating fire from 8,000 Polygars, who constantly pressed upon our advanced party, rushed upon the line of attack, piked the bullocks that were dragging the guns, and killed many of our people. But these attempts were repulsed by perseverance, and before sunset we had opened a passage entirely to the mountain; it is extremely high, rocky, and in many places almost perpendicular. Having resolved to attack from this unexpected quarter, the troops undertook the service and attained the summit. The Polygar parties posted to guard that eminence, being routed, after much firing on all hands, we descended on the other side and flanked the Comby. The enemy seeing us masters of the mountain, retreated under cover of the night, by paths inaccessible to regular troops, and we took possession of the wonderful recess. The particulars respecting ordnance, stores and provisions, found in the place, are stated in my letter of the third of September*. We left the third and ninth bat-

* See Letter of the third of September, in the Appendix.

talions to ſecure the magazines, and moved the army to Shevlepatore within four marches of Madura, in order to awe the northern Polygars of Tinivelly.

It was little more than a month ſince we had left Tritchinopoly. Your authority was re-eſtabliſhed throughout the whole track that we had traverſed, extending more than 300 miles: and beſides the arrangement with the Shevigunga Rajah, we were maſters of the two ſtrongeſt places belonging to the Polygars. We remained ſome time in expectation of their propoſing a general accommodation, but they knew that Tippoo ſtill inveſted Mangalore, and that we muſt quickly join the force at Dindigul. This intelligence corroborated their ſpirit of procraſtination. I therefore convened the Vakeels*, whom the chief Polygars had ſent to treat with me in camp, and directed them to inform their

* Vakeels are deputies, agents, or ambaſſadors.

reſpective

respective principals, that we should leave the province on the twenty-first of September; adding, that if they did not return to their allegiance, I should make a vow to Siven, the Gentoo god whose attribute is *vengeance*, to march back and spread destruction throughout every possession of the defaulting Polygars: this declaration alarmed the whole assembly. My letters to Mr. Irwin expressed my regret on leaving the province before any settlement was concluded with the Polygars; and in return he forwarded to me the terms on which he thought it expedient to restore their forts to Catabominaigue and Shevigerry.

Vakeels from these chiefs waited on me at Trimungulum*, and stipulated, in the name of their masters, that they would pay thirty thousand chuckrums† each, in

* Trimungulum is fifteen miles south-west of Madura.

† A chuckrum is somewhat less than a pagoda.

 lieu

lieu of all preceding claims. They likewise gave their bonds for fifteen thousand pagodas, or 6,000*l.* each, in consideration of the restitution of their forts. Obligations were farther exacted, that the defences of Pandalamcourchy should be demolished, that the guns, stores, and ammunition should be removed to Palamcottah; that the road which we cleared to the Comby of Shevigerry should continue open; that the means of defence should be removed from the place, and that the southern commanders, and the Company's troops, should at all times be admitted within their forts and barriers: I concluded with injunctions to observe a more submissive conduct, if they valued their lives, property, or posterity. As soon as the restitution of the forts and prisoners* could possibly take place, the third and ninth battalions

* Among the prisoners there was a daughter of Catabominaigue, who, as well as all the others, amounting to many hundreds, were treated with the utmost attention.

under

under Captain Mackinnon, were directed to march from Shevigerry, and to join the force at Dindigul, whither the army proceeded by the route of Madura.

Your Lordſhip and the Board are not unacquainted with the unworthy practices by which the fertile province of Tinivelly has ſuffered ſince the diſreputable expedition thither under Maphuze Cawn and Colonel Heron. Their defeat by the Nat Coleries near Madura was not more diſgraceful, than the principles upon which that and ſubſequent armaments againſt the Polygars have been conducted. Though clear ſtatements and ſpecific charges, leaving no retroſpect of exaction, together with ſimplicity of arrangement, and diſpatch in execution, are the great barriers againſt malverſation, the oppoſite of ſuch conduct conſtantly prevailed; until your Lordſhip and the Board aſſumed the management of thoſe territories, nothing was definite—nothing was con-

concluded; partial payments were received; paſt claims were left for future ſettlement; many months were waſted in fitting out an expedition, and ſtill more in performing ſlight ſervices. During the whole period of protraction, the Renter, the Amuldar, the Phouzdar, and the European commander, were reaping the harveſt of corruption, and ſowing for an after-growth of peculation. The Polygars are ſubtle and acute:—they took advantage of ſo corrupt a ſyſtem;—and, notwithſtanding their internal feuds, they united againſt a common invader. They adminiſtered to the avarice of their opponent by bribes, and to his paſſion for command by procraſtination. Thus the province was impaired,—its cultivation failed,—its manufactures diminiſhed;—every new Collector and Commander entailed new evils, and taught the Polygars to conſider their peſhcuſh* not as a juſt tribute to their ſove-

* Peſhcuſh is the ſum paid by thoſe who hold of a ſuperior.

ſovereign, but as a price to purchaſe the forbearance of oppreſſors.

The conduct of Mahomed Iſſoof Cawn deſerves to be exempted from this general accuſation. While he ruled thoſe provinces, his whole adminiſtration denoted vigour and effect: his juſtice was unqueſtioned,— his word unalterable,—his meaſures were happily combined, and firmly executed;— the guilty had no refuge from puniſhment: his maxim was, that the labourer and the manufacturer ſhould be the favourite children of the Circar, becauſe they afford ſtrength and comfort to the public parent; but that the Polygar and the Collery, though equally entitled to truth and juſtice, have no pretenſion to indulgence, becauſe they are the worthleſs prodigals who waſte their own means and ravage thoſe of others. "Let them become Zemindars," ſaid he, "and cultivate their own lands, inſtead of "plundering their induſtrious neighbours; "then

"then they ſhall be cheriſhed: but while "their habit is idleneſs, and their buſineſs "devaſtation, I will treat every one as a "public enemy, who wields a pike, or "wears the turban of a Polygar." On comparing the ſtate of that country with his conduct and remarks, I found that wiſdom, vigour, and integrity were never more conſpicuous in any perſon of whatever climate or complexion.

On my arrival at Dindigul, an order of encampment was tranſmitted to your Board in two lines*, containing one European and three Sepoy brigades, beſides four flank battalions that acted as a fifth brigade. Our artillery conſiſted of ſixty-five pieces of cannon with field-ammunition, and 10,000 battering ſhot; the engineers' department was ſtored with beſieging tools and other implements; the pioneer corps was ſtrengthened; the cavalry, excepting three troops, were natives and irregulars; they amounted

* See the annexed Plate.

to

to 1000 men, and ſerved to flank the baggage on the line of march. The Commiſſary of Stores department, including the conveyance of artillery, required a numerous retinue of draught and carriage cattle: theſe we had for ſeveral months uſed unremitting efforts to procure; and by the aſſiſtance of Mr. Sulivan, Mr. Irwin, and Mr. Johnſton, in addition to our own exertions, we aſſembled a greater number of bullocks than ever were attached to any Engliſh force in India.

The Agent Victualler was obliged to convey arrack and proviſions for 2000 Europeans. But the buſineſs of the Grain-keeper was ſtill more embarraſſing; where 14,000 fighting men and many thouſand public followers* were to be ſubſiſted, without money or other means of ſupply, except

* The public followers conſiſt of Laſcars for the tents, drivers of bullocks, artificers, and doolymen to carry the ſick and wounded.

ſuch

ſuch magazines of the enemy as we were enabled to reduce. It had been the uſage of Indian commanders to levy duties on all articles bought or ſold in the bazar or market of the army. Under whatever ſanction this cuſtom took its riſe, it is an odious tax upon the ſoldier for the benefit of his ſuperior.——I permitted no ſuch practice.

Another material object was the mode and order of marching.—The practice on the coaſt has been to form the Sepoy corps three deep, and the Europeans two deep, and then to move by files with a ſtrong advance guard, and a ſtill ſtronger rear guard, in order to cover the carts and other wheeled conveyances that follow the line: the baggage is then diſpoſed of on the right or left flank, according to the nature of the ground over which the army is to paſs, and covered by a ſtrong force, to repel the rapid charges of the enemy's cavalry.

It

It is asserted that many benefits attend this mode in India; that if the line is attacked on either flank, it is enabled to form with much celerity by a simple movement of conversion; and that if a charge be made in front or rear, the corps have only to advance, or countermarch and form a front to the attack. But a large army marching by files is many miles in length, consequently there is little communication between distant parts of the line; neither can a Commander observe the whole extent, or know the state of different divisions. If in marching by files, a movement to the front or rear is necessary in line of battle or by corps, much time is lost in the manœuvre, and in the precautions requisite in the face of an enemy. The Carnatic army, adhering to this principle, have frequently been cannonaded many hours before they could form the line for action.

To

To remedy theſe evils I propoſed to form the army into five diviſions, and to diſpoſe them in ſhape of what in another ſcience is called a quincunx. The European brigade being uſually placed in the centre of the line, ſhould form the centre diviſion of the quincunx, with a Sepoy brigade in front, another in the rear, and one on each flank: the battering train and baggage to move under cover of the diviſion leaſt likely to be charged; and the brigades to move, not by files, but in columns, and at ſuch diſtances, that whenever it may be neceſſary to form the line to the front, flank, or rear, the centre brigade, and that which is to become the right and left wings, may occupy the whole intermediate ſpace. Thus, if the line be attacked in front, the centre brigade and the two flank brigades immediately form a line to the front, and the advance and rear brigades take their ſtations either as a ſecond line, as a baggage-guard

and

and a reserve, or to extend the main line. If the line be attacked, or if it be meant to attack on the right or left flanks, the centre brigades, with the front and rear brigades, face to the right and left, and form the line, while the two brigades that were the flank divisions on the line of march are posted as circumstances may require. Thus, in every possible point of attack, the line is quickly formed, the baggage protected, and the army prepared for action.

Your instructions of the 18th of August directed me to remain on the frontiers, ready to act offensively, in case of an infraction on the part of Tippoo Sultaun; and for this purpose, the army moved to re-occupy Daraporam. We found that the magazines which we left there in June had been greatly consumed; but there still remained a fortnight's subsistence for the troops.

From the ultimate object of a movement to the capital of Myſore, we had never deviated. Guns, ſhot, and ſtores, had been collected from the ſouthern garriſons, and numerous artificers were employed on our carriages and conveyance. The zeal of Mr. Sulivan, Mr. Irwin, and Mr. Hippiſley, had forwarded our views; and the Rajah of Travancore had been ſolicited for an advance of ſtores, in the event of our moving againſt the ſouthern poſſeſſions of Tippoo Sultaun. This could not fail to coincide with the wiſhes of the Rajah, which induced him to ſupport Colonel Humberſtone on the Malabar coaſt during the preceding year, and to reinforce his army with ſeveral battalions.

A conſtant correſpondence was alſo carried on with the Zamorin, or ancient ſovereign of Callcut, and the other Rajahs on the Malabar ſide of the peninſula who were diſaffected to the Myſorean uſurpation; and

no

no circumſtance was omitted that appeared conducive to the important operation which we had ſo earneſtly in view: but although the army had acquired ſtrength and efficiency, yet we poſſeſſed not that fulneſs of equipment which cannot be accompliſhed with an empty treaſury. Tanjore and Tritchinopoly had not yet recovered from the calamities which they had experienced: the Marawas and Tinivelly were new in their allegiance. Thoſe countries therefore, far from affording ſufficient payments for the army, could hardly be ſuppoſed competent, under ſuch circumſtances, to defray the current charges of their garriſons, although the wiſe arrangements of your ſuperintendants gave us every reaſon to expect a rapid increaſe of revenue.

The gentlemen who zealouſly ſupplied us with ſtores and conveyance, were obliged to employ their perſonal credit, truſting to the future ſolvency of Government: the

 native

native troops were twelve months in arrear: our ordnance, though numerous, was of inconvenient calibers: the carriages had suffered by our continued marching: gunney-bags for carrying rice, copper hoops for powder-barrels, cordage for dragging the guns across a country unexplored by armies, and various other articles in the Commissary of Stores' department, were deficient indeed, when compared with the supplies that the Carnatic army daily received from the Presidency. Above all, the want of money rendered it impossible to pay the Head Black Men, who had employed bullocks in the service for such a length of time, that their private funds were exhausted, and their faith in the Company impaired.

During former wars there ever had been frequent payments to the troops, which enabled them to procure supplies from the traders and inhabitants, even in the enemy's country. Under these circumstances, the con-

conveyance of many days provision was not indispensably required: whereas the want of magazines and money left us no security of subsistence, except the grain we could carry with us, or seize as we advanced: for this purpose statements were procured of the grain deposited within two hundred miles of our front and flank; and several hundred people were employed on that and other business of intelligence.

It was farther necessary, not only to conceal our own intentions, but to discover those of the enemy; for want of similar precautions, three English armies had been cut off or taken prisoners in India.

As no one Harcarrah can possibly keep pace with the rapid movements of the Mysore cavalry, confidential intelligencers were established at every considerable town in the Mysore dominions, as well as in the enemy's camp, and in the Durbars of the Ra-

 jahs

jahs inimical to Tippoo Sultaun. On the first notice of any material incident, these intelligencers dispatched small cadjeans*, which were more rapidly conveyed to me than any horse could travel, by Tappals or relays of Colleries, stationed at moderate distances, and unsuspected by the enemy. Harcarrahs, Peons, lubby-merchants, and Sepoys were also constantly traversing all parts of the enemy's country; others, carrying dispatches to Madras and the southern provinces, to Travancore, to Cochin, to the Malabar Rajahs, to General Macleod at Cannanore, to Colonel Campbell at Mangalore, and to the Residency at Telicherry. The intelligence of every individual was carefully registered, and tended to confirm or to refute the various intimations constantly arriving. By these means, during many months of continued marching through a country almost unexplored, we never once

* Cadjeans are thick leaves, resembling the papyrus, on which the Gentoos write.

failed in our ſupplies, nor did any material incident eſcape our knowledge.

The diſcretionary powers with which your Board inveſted me, rendered it my peculiar duty to conſider the mode of warfare moſt likely to diſtreſs the enemy. The ſyſtem of a war in India, which is to depend on field operations, muſt ever be expoſed to diſappointment. In the war of 1767, General J. Smith purſued Hyder's army in a ſeries of rapid marches, in order to bring him to a deciſive action; but Hyder, after leading him through the Myſore country in various directions, marched paſt our army to Madras *, and intimidated the Government into a diſreputable treaty.

It was obvious that our circumſtances did not admit of war on ſuch conditions: that ſtrong forts muſt be reduced, territories poſ-

* Before this event took place, General J. Smith was called to the Preſidency, and the army was commanded by Colonel Fitzgerald.

 ſeſſed,

ſeſſed, their magazines and revenues render-ed productive; and that we muſt proceed by unexpected ſtrides, to ſuch poſitions as might preſerve a communication with our own provinces, forming at the ſame time regular ſtages towards the capital of Myſore. This implied that we were to act on the principles of a beſieging army, to make lodgments as we advanced, and ſtill to preſs forward; to diminiſh the reſources of the enemy, while we increaſed our own; to oblige him, either to ſuffer us to proceed unmoleſted in the proſecution of operations, of which the ultimate object was the overthrow of his government, or elſe to compel him, in the obſtruction of theſe proceedings, to afford us the wiſhed-for opportunity of a cloſe engagement in the field. Such was the ſyſtem on which I propoſed to act, truſting that the inefficiency of the oppoſite or field ſyſtem, as evinced in the conduct of the war of 1767, and in the late Carnatic war, would be held ſufficient to induce a change

change of meaſures; for an army conſtituted as Hyder's, with a ſuperabundance of elephants, camels, bullocks, and cavalry, muſt out-march an army formed of infantry like ours,—unqualified by principle and formation to commit the devaſtation of a Maratta or Myſorean army. Our field operations are neither alarming to the enemy, nor productive of advantage to our own cauſe; and our forces, when conſtituted for field operations only, paſs through a country, and leave no veſtige of their ſervices.

On the fourth of October I repreſented our alarming ſituation, in caſe Tippoo Sultaun ſhould leave us long in a ſtate of uncertainty; and added, that to remain upon the frontiers, in expectation of events, would be impoſſible, for we could not hope to procure more than a month's proviſion within the diſtrict: that to fall back upon the Company's ſouthern poſſeſſions, would

frustrate

frustrate your intentions, and exhaust the produce of those countries. Besides, so large an army unpaid and unemployed, is ever at the mercy of the first incident that may occasion discontent. These considerations induced me to solicit from your Lordship and the Board, a latitude of purveyance, even in the enemy's country, in case his protractions should endanger the safety of the troops, so critically situated.

On the sixteenth of October the army marched towards Pylny, about thirty miles south of Daraporam, in order to put the renter of Dindigul's family in possession of their inheritance, or petty Rajahship of Pylny. They assured me of grain and cattle at that place; and this was the last resource we had to expect, without advancing into the enemy's country, or falling back on the southern provinces. Most fortunately, while impressed with the approach of these impending difficulties, an official

official letter from Meff. Frith and Patterfon, members of the refidency of Telicherry, informed me of a re-commencement of hoftility, on the part of Tippoo Sultaun, againft Mangalore. I confequently held myfelf bound by your inftructions of the eighteenth of Auguft, to take immediate meafures to refent the infraction.

On the eighteenth of October it became my duty to inform your Board, of the embarraffments under which we laboured, and to intimate my intention of moving in full force to the weftward. The immediate object of this movement was the relief of Mangalore: the ultimate object was, the reduction of Hyder's family, or at leaft the attainment of a refpectable accommodation. Our expectation of relieving Mangalore, by an actual appearance before the place, was exceedingly remote; for we had not lefs than 500 miles of an enemy's country to traverfe. There appeared

appeared but two practicable movements of sufficient moment to make Tippoo raise the siege of Mangalore: the one was, to move by Coimbatour, Settimungulum, and the pass of Gudjereddy, which leads up the ghauts or mountains on which the kingdom of Mysore is elevated, directly to Mysore fort and Seringapatam: the other was, to move against Palagatcherry.

The design I had formed of moving to Tippoo's capital, with a view of forming a permanent establishment, has been already stated. For this purpose, an intermediate place of strength and resources was required, to serve as a magazine of stores and provisions for the prosecution of our undertakings, or to secure a retreat if necessary. Neither Coimbatour, though the capital of a rich Rajahship, nor Settimungulum, nor Ardenelli, which are the principal forts in the direct road from Daraporam to the city of Seringapatam, were of sufficient strength

ſtrength to juſtify our truſting any of them as our main depoſit. For the unexpected loſs of ſuch a magazine, while the army might be ſeveral hundred miles advanced in an enemy's country, ſurrounded by a formidable force, might have ſubjected us to diſaſters, of which the Engliſh armies, defeated and taken priſoners during the war, were melancholy remembrancers.

Palagatcherry held forth every advantage, being a place of the firſt ſtrength in India, while its territory afforded a ſuperabundance of proviſion *. The mountains that bound the paſs which it commands, are ſtrengthened by thick foreſts and ſurrounding woods; and the interſections of the Paniani river, through deep rice grounds, concurred to enable a ſmall body of infantry to defend

* Palagatcherry was completely rebuilt by Hyder ſince the war of 1767 with the Engliſh, and was furniſhed with all the advantages of European conſtruction and defence.

the

the territory against any number of horse. It farther commanded the only practicable communication between the coasts of Coromandel and Malabar, and promised us possession of all the countries from Tritchinopoly by Daraporam, in a track of more than 200 miles.—It opened the means of supply from Travancore, Cochin, and other places on the Malabar coast.—It afforded confidence to the Zamorin, and other disaffected Rajahs, from Cochin to Goa, who were struggling to shake off the yoke of Hyder.—It left us at liberty to disguise our movements, and to proceed either by the route of Coimbatour and Gudjereddy, or by Calicut on the Malabar sea, and the pass of Damalcherry, to the siege of Seringapatam.—It was besides of such intrinsic consequence to the Mysore Government, that the reduction of it could not fail to weigh essentially in the negotiations for peace then said to be in agitation, and promised to make Tippoo

Sultaun

Sultaun raiſe the ſiege of Mangalore in order to oppoſe our further progreſs.

We advanced from Pylny on the twenty-ſecond of October, reduced the forts of Cumalum, Chuckligerry, and Annamalley, and paſſed through a rich country, abounding with dry grain *, cattle, wood, and rice fields. At Palatchy the ground attains its higheſt elevation, and the ſtreams run eaſt and weſt to the Coromandel and Malabar ſeas. During our whole march through this part of the country, the flank brigade under Captain Maitland, moved conſtantly in front, occupied poſitions, and ſecured proviſions for the army.

From Annamalley our progreſs became truly laborious, being obliged to force our way through a foreſt twenty miles in depth, extending thirty miles acroſs the paſs of Pa-

* Dry grain is that which grows without flooding the land, cholum, natchenny, cambo, gram, doll, &c. whereas rice requires at certain ſeaſons to be under water.

lagat.

lagat. Our object was to reach Colingoody, a post on the western side of the forest, within fifteen miles of Palagatcherry. The frequent ravines required to be filled up before it was possible to drag the guns across them,—innumerable large trees which obstructed the passage, required to be cut down and drawn out of the intended track, and then the whole road was to be formed, before the carriages could pass. The brigades were distributed to succeed each other at intervals, preceded by pioneers, in order to clear what the advanced body had opened for the guns and stores that were to move under cover of the rear division.

While we were thus engaged, an unremitting rain, extremely unusual at that season, commenced. The ravines were filled with water,—the paths became slippery,—the bullocks lost their footing,—and the troops were obliged to drag the guns and carriages across the whole forest. I forced on with the advance to Colingoody, in order to make the neceſſary arrangements with the people of the Zamorin; who had prepared for the future ſubſiſtence of the army. The diſpoſitions of the inhabitants towards us, and their means of ſupply, exceeded our moſt ſanguine expectations. The Zamorin's Vakeel informed the Bramins, that we were friends to their cauſe, and earneſt to deliver them from the yoke of Hyder; that we only wiſhed to receive the public proportion of the grain, but none from individuals; and that any perſon belonging to the camp who ſhould attempt to plunder, would be hanged in front of the lines. On hearing theſe declarations, they teſtified the ſtrongeſt ſatisfaction; and their confidence increaſed when they found that the firſt offenders were executed.——The rains continuing fourteen days without intermiſſion, the paſſage through the foreſt became daily more diſtreſsful, and the troops were expoſed in their whole pro-

M greſs,

grefs, without the poffibility of pitching tents, or of procuring for them either cover or convenience.

Colingoody is fifteen miles from Palagatcherry, and the road lies entirely through rice grounds, with interfecting ridges covered with cocoa and other trees. The water and embankments neceffary for the cultivation of rice, render it difficult for guns to pafs, and impracticable for cavalry to act. As foon as a fufficient force got through the wood, the advanced corps moved to the bank* of the Paniani river, within random fhot of the works of Palagatcherry, where we took a fecure pofition, and prepared to inveft the place. My Bramin Harcarrahs † had executed a model of the fort in clay, a work at which they are extremely dexterous; and on all hands we had received accounts of it that appeared

* November 2d.

† Harcarrahs are people who give intelligence, fhow roads, &c.

exag-

exaggerated; but a near inſpection of its ſtrength impreſſed me with ſerious apprehenſions that much time might be waſted in its reduction.

On the fourth of November, the main body of the troops, not including the rear diviſion, arrived at our poſition on the river, which we paſſed next day, and encamped about two miles eaſt from the fort, acroſs the great road that leads from Combatour. The engineers' ſtores arrived, and a poſt for them was eſtabliſhed, where all the preparations for a ſiege were collected. As our next object was, to circumſcribe the beſieged, and accelerate our approaches, with this view we occupied the pettah, or open town, on the eaſt and north faces of the fort: and on each of theſe faces carried forward an attack. During the whole period of our approaches, and in the conſtruction of our trenches, parallels, and batteries, the beſieged kept a continued fire on our covering and

 working

working parties. The battering train and ftores, however, under cover of the fourth brigade, reached our encampment on the 9th, after a fucceffion of toil that would appear incredible if recited in detail.

Apprehending much delay from the ftrength of the works, and the obftinacy of the defenders, efpecially if they fhould force us to approach by fap to the creft of the glacis, and to proceed from thence by regular gradations acrofs the ditch, we refolved at a feafonable opportunity to attempt the gateway. We found it fo ftrongly flanked and fortified, that it appeared almoft fecure from any attack; however, having no drawbridge, we founded our hopes of accelerating the fiege on this circumftance. We did not therefore permit any heavy metal whatever to be fired till the thirteenth, when we opened with twelve guns and four howitzers from two batteries at 400 yards diftance from the eaft and north faces of the fort, and

and before ſunſet the defences were ſo much damaged, that the fire of the beſieged conſiderably abated.

The particulars of our attack, and the ſurrender of the place during the night, which are explained at full length in my letter of the 15th of November, were not more fortunate than unexpected. We found the fort covered by a reſpectable glacis, with a good covertway; a very broad and deep ditch, completely reveted; a large berme, and a very ſtrong commanding rampart. The figure of the fort was nearly quadrangular: the dimenſions of its faces were 528 feet by 432: each angle was defended by a capacious round baſtion with nine embraſures, and a baſtion of a ſimilar conſtruction on the centre of each curtain. It had only one entrance, paſſing through three gateways, mounted a great number of guns upon the works, and contained a garriſon of 4000 men.

On the night of the thirteenth, Captain Maitland, with a part of the four flank battalions, took the advantage of a heavy rain to drive the besieged from the covert-way. Being so fortunate as to succeed, he pursued them within the first and as far as the second gateway, where he was stopped, but maintained his ground with great spirit and ability until a reinforcement arrived. This mode of attack so much alarmed the enemy, that they called out for quarter, and put us in possession of a fort capable of making a long and desperate resistance. We found 50,000 pagodas in the place, besides a very large supply of grain, guns, powder, shot, and military stores.

In my letters to your Lordship and the Board on this subject, it appeared necessary for me to be minute in a description of the place, because its consequence and local situation were not accurately known to Europeans. This fortress commands

mands a fertile and extenſive diſtrict, the adjacent foreſts abound with the fineſt Teek timber* in India, and the river Paniani is at hand to float it to the Malabar ſea. Palagatcherry, from its poſition, equally menaces the poſſeſſions of Tippoo on the weſtern coaſt and towards Myſore by the route of Combatour and Gudjereddy; while the movements of the ſouthern army, almoſt without money or ſubſiſtence, except what we procured on our march, afford ſufficient proof, that magazines of grain eſtabliſhed there would enable armies to penetrate with confidence and ſecurity from the coaſt of Coromandel to that of Malabar, and thus bring the military reſources of Madras and Bombay into one point of union and effect.

On the ſurrender of Palagatcherry, the place was garriſoned by the nineteenth

* Teek timber is equal, if not ſuperior, to Oak for the purpoſes of ſhipbuilding. There is likewiſe a great quantity of Sandal-wood in the neighbourhood.

battalion, with a few Europeans and ſome irregulars under Captain Dewar, one of your ableſt officers. The heir apparent of the Zamorin left his retirement in the woods, and remained with me during the ſiege. In anſwer to his urgent ſolicitations, that we ſhould reſtore him to the dominions of which Hyder had deprived his family, I declared, that in the event of our moving by Calicut, we might hope to effect his re-eſtabliſhment there; and that in the mean while he ſhould be reinſtated in the territory of Palagat, an ancient dependency of the Zamorins,—requiring only from him, that he ſhould furniſh grain for the army while in that vicinity, without any other obligation, until the concluſion of the war, or until your Government ſhould make ſome regular agreement with him.

To eſtabliſh more fully the Zamorin's authority, and to afford him the neceſſary ſupport in his preſent ſituation, a large

large body of Bramin Harcarrahs, who had conſtantly remained with me in camp, were employed, and proved not only of great ſervice in the buſineſs of intelligence, but of material influence in conciliating the Gentoos. Accompanied by them, we frequently rode through the adjacent villages, aſſembled the head people, and aſſured them of protection. During theſe proceedings I maintained a correſpondence with Brigadier General Macleod, Colonel Campbell, and the Reſidency of Telicherry, intimating my intention of approaching their coaſt, and aſſuring General Macleod of my earneſt wiſh to co-operate with him in every meaſure that could tend to advance us in full force againſt Seringapatam. Having heard that there was abundance of battering guns and military ſtores at Telicherry, I wrote for ſuch ſupplies as could be ſpared, offering to move down to Paniani or Calicut, and to proceed to Seringapatam, either by the paſs of Damalcherry, through the country of our

our friends the Nyars, or elſe to return from Paniani or Calicut to Palagatcherry, and from thence by Coimbatour, as he might judge moſt eligible.

The Admiral Sir Edward Hughes being then at Telicherry with the ſquadron, I entreated him to ſend a veſſel with ſtores to Paniani, and, in order to guard againſt diſappointment, diſpatched meſſengers to Cochin, to ſecure an ample ſupply at that place. General Macleod with his diſtinguiſhed liberality of character aſſured me, that in the event of my moving towards him, he would unite in proſecuting the movement to Seringapatam, without taking any advantage of his ſeniority, and without interfering in the command of the ſouthern army. Finding, however, that his army could not be put in motion in leſs than two months, for want of bullocks and conveyance; that no ſubſtantial ſtock of military ſtores could be expected at Telicherry;

and that we ſhould meet with extreme obſtruction in our progreſs through the deep and interſected routes leading from Palagatcherry to Calicut; we reſolved to rely on Cochin for ſupplies, and to proſecute our meaſures by Coimbatour, ſtill preſerving the utmoſt union of operation with the Malabar army.

We arrived before Coimbatour on the twenty-ſixth of November, having been annoyed with rockets on the march, by a very large body of horſe. Finding that there was no glacis, we proceeded immediately to erect a battery, but before we had effected a breach, the Killidar* ſurrendered; and on this occaſion we treated him and his garriſon with the utmoſt kindneſs, as we had before done thoſe of Daraporam and Palagatcherry. A great quantity of ammunition, ſtores, and grain, were found in the fort; and the adjacent grounds were co-

* Commander of the fort.

vered

vered with abundant crops. The poſſeſſion of this town, being the capital of the greateſt antient Rajahſhip in the country, promiſed eminent advantage; for although not remarkable on account of its military ſtrength, it is held in higher eſtimation than any other place belonging to the Myſoreans in the Payen Ghaut, or country below the mountains.

We now arrive at the moſt intereſting moment of the war. The garriſon of Mangalore, under its ineſtimable commander Colonel Campbell, had made a defence that has been ſeldom equalled and never ſurpaſſed. With a handful of men worn out by fatigue and famine, he reſiſted for many months a formidable army under Tippoo Sultaun. The whole power of that prince, aſſiſted by the ſcience of his French auxiliaries, could not force a breach that had long lain open, and he was repulſed in every attempt to carry it by ſtorm.

Tippoo's

Tippoo's army, particularly the cavalry, had suffered greatly by a perseverance in the siege during the whole period of the rainy season. The interior affairs of his dominions, being unsettled since his recent accession, were in extreme confusion. His failure against Mangalore had encouraged the Corga Rajah, a powerful Chief under the mountains that separate the Malabar country from Mysore, to assert independency by arms; while every other ancient Rajah on the Malabar side of India from Goa to Cochin, was eager to repel the tyranny of the Mysore Government, to which the whole of that extensive coast no longer owned subjection.

General Macleod at the head of the Malabar forces, strong in Europeans, artillery, and native corps, supported these Rajahs, and laboured with his usual energy to complete the system that he had materially promoted. There was likewise a force acting

acting under General Jones, against the Cudapah country, or northern possessions of Tippoo Sultaun, where his power was ill established; and the army under my direction was perhaps the strongest force belonging to Europeans that had ever been employed in India. The countries we had reduced extended 200 miles in length, from the district of Tritchinopoly on the east, to Ramgarry, thirty miles west of Palagatcherry, afforded provisions for 100,000 men, and yielded an annual revenue of 600,000*l.*, while every necessary arrangement had been made for the regular collection of these resources.

The fort and pass of Palagatcherry secured our western flank, and the intermediate position of General Macleod's army between that place and Tippoo's main army at Mangalore, together with the singular combination of ravines, rivers and embankments that intersect the Malabar countries,

tries, and the mountains that divide them from Myſore, through which the paſſes were occupied by our friends the diſaffected Rajahs, rendered it almoſt impracticable for Tippoo to move in that direction againſt our new acquiſitions. To attack them by a movement through the paſſes of the Ghauts, on the eaſtern flank towards Salem and Erode, ſuppoſed a circuit of five or ſix hundred miles from the poſition of Tippoo's army before Mangalore. His movements therefore againſt theſe acquiſitions could only be attempted by the central paſs from Myſore at Gudjereddy, which is not fifty miles in front from Coimbatour: and the poſſeſſion of that paſs aſſured us an immediate acceſs to the capital of Tippoo's kingdom, commanding a communication with our new acquiſitions, and with the Company's ſouthern provinces. Beſides, as far as the ſyſtem of defending front flanks and rear can ever be extended from the poſition of an army to the topographical

cal circumſtances of a country, it would enable us to ſecure thoſe territories from any conſiderable irruptions. At this period too, the chumba or great crop throughout the country was upon the ground, and, independently of the magazines in our front, promiſed ample proviſion.

The Corga Rajah had repeatedly promiſed us ſupplies from his country, extending within thirty miles of Seringapatam. Theſe promiſes were confirmed by the Zamorin, who had abundantly furniſhed us with grain at Palagatcherry. This Prince likewiſe engaged for the aſſiſtance of all the Malabar Chiefs, commanding the ghauts or mountains that bound Myſore upon the weſt; and convinced us that they were not only willing to provide for us during the ſiege, but to form magazines in ſtrong poſitions among the mountains, and to join us with 20 or 30,000 Nyars if required.

Mahomed

Mahomed Ally, and other diſtinguiſhed leaders, had been executed in the camp of Tippoo, for exciting diſaffection. A recent conſpiracy had occurred in Seringapatam, menacing the releaſement of the Engliſh priſoners, the excluſion of Tippoo's family, and the re-eſtabliſhment of the antient Rana, or Gentoo ſovereign of Myſore. In addition to this enumeration of advantages, we had every reaſon to rely on the Gentoo or Canara race forming the great maſs of inhabitants in Myſore, who had unequivocal proofs of my earneſt zeal to ſupport their intereſts and favourite family; while every circumſtance of preſent ſituation or of future proſpect ſeemed to mark this intereſting moment as the criſis of the war.

The troops were immediately provided with ten days grain, the carriages repaired, the departments arranged, and the army prepared to march. My deſign againſt the

 forts

forts and magazines of Settimungulum and Ardenelli *, was communicated to your Board; and from thence it was my intention to push forward to the city of Seringapatam with the utmost rapidity that could be united with precaution. Exulting in the bright perspective that lay before us, we felt a painful eagerness for the moment of departure; our expectations, however, of restoring the English name and consequence in India were of short duration.

Your Lordship and the Board had judged it expedient to delegate your powers of negotiation to commissioners, who were to treat of peace at the Durbar of Tippoo Sultaun. Invested with full authority by your Board to give what instructions they thought proper to all troops of the English em-

* Settimungulum is situated on the banks of the Caveri, below the pass of Gudjerreddy. Ardenelli stands on the top of the ghauts, on the elevated flat or table land of Mysore.

ployed

ployed against the Mysoreans, they proceeded to the camp of Mudeen ul Deen Cawn near Arnee in the Carnatic. Between that place and Atcherry Waukum they received intelligence, that in consequence of information from the Residency of Telicherry, intimating to me a renewal of hostility on the part of Tippoo Sultaun against Mangalore, the army under my command had moved into the enemy's country, and had reduced Palagatcherry. After many compliments to my own conduct and exertions, they directed me forthwith to restore all posts, forts, and countries lately reduced, and to retire within the limits possessed by the English on the twenty-sixth of the preceding July. This letter reached me on the twenty-eighth of November, two days before my intended march towards Gudjereddy and Seringapatam. Neither feeling myself at liberty to disregard an order so peremptorily conveyed, nor to fulfil the utmost extent of its literal signification, I stated

ſtated to them the benefits of our poſition, and the menacing appearance on the Malabar coaſt; tranſmitting at the ſame time ſimilar communications to your Board, and intimating my intention of remaining at Coimbatour until I ſhould be farther inſtructed. My Aid de Camp, Captain Moody, with the ſame view, proceeded to Madras; and was fully qualified by knowledge and ability to explain our ſituation, and to prove that a movement to Seringapatam would endanger the throne of Hyder.

During the ſucceeding interval, every moment was employed in adding to the fulneſs of our equipment. Rochin Cawn, the commander of Tippoo's army in the country of Coimbatour, was informed, that we would obſerve the ceſſation till further orders*. Captain Maitland, with the flank

* Habits of intercourſe took place between Rochin Cawn's camp and ours, of which there had been no example between contending armies in India.

brigade,

brigade, proceeded to Dindigul and Tanjore, in order to bring supplies of stores from the southern garrisons. Mr. Digby, Paymaster in camp, whose zeal and public talents have on all occasions been conspicuous, went to procure money at Tinivelly, and to concert with Mr. Irwin, Superintendant there, a permanent mode of remittance and supply: and as soon as this reinforcement should be ready to move towards us, it was my intention to fall back and cover the junction. In the mean time the third brigade was detached by Palagatcherry to Cochin, where the Governor had prepared for us a considerable stock of arrack, stores, and ammunition; while the main body of the army remained at Coimbatour, ready to oppose the enemy. But these and all similar arrangements were rendered abortive by your minutes of consultation dated the fifth of December, directing me to fulfil the order of unqualified restitution enjoined by your Deputies, as the preliminaries of negotiation

 with

with Tippoo Sultaun. These papers reached me about the middle of December, and a few days afterwards I received from the Commissioners another letter, repeating their instructions.

We had entirely consumed the grain in Coimbatour, and all that was ripe in the adjacent fields. We were not at liberty to move in our intended course, nor to look for new supplies, which would have been considered as an infraction of the cessation; it therefore became necessary to return to Palagatcherry, where the troops received grain to subsist them as far as Tritchinopoly and Madura, a distance of two hundred miles. On the twenty-eighth of December, the army advanced towards the southern countries; and at the same time three battalions under Captain Wheeler were detached to escort the stores from Cochin, with directions to evacuate Palagatcherry, and to join us by the route of Annamalley and Pylny, close to the

the mountains. On our second march we were visited by the Rev. Mr. Swartz, whom your Lordship and the Board requested to proceed to Seringapatam as a faithful interpreter between Tippoo and the Commissioners. The knowledge and integrity of this irreproachable Missionary have retrieved the character of Europeans from imputations of general depravity. A respectable escort attended him to the nearest encampment of the enemy; but he was stopped at Settimungulum, and returned to Tanjore. I rejoice, however, that he undertook the business; for his journal which has been before your Board evinces, that the southern army acted towards our enemies with a mildness seldom experienced by friends in moments of pacification. From him also you learned, that this conduct operated on the minds of the inhabitants, who declared that we afforded them more secure protection than the commanders of their own troops.

 The

The army had now been fed for many months entirely at the expence of the enemy; and directions were given, that all grain found in the country should be served out to the troops in lieu of batta *, thereby saving to the Company an advance of nearly 500 *l.* per day for the whole time the army was so subsisted, and leaving the troops to make their after-claims, in case they should expect to receive that grain on the footing of capture †.

On the fourth of January 1784, the army arrived at Ayryacotta. Colonel Stuart with the main division proceeded to

* Batta is the extra sum allowed to troops over and above their pay, in lieu of subsistence while in the field.

† Some other armies had charged the Company with the batta due to every soldier in the field, notwithstanding that a sufficiency of grain had been seized for the maintenance of the troops. Thus the amount of the grain found was diverted from public saving to the benefit of individuals. If I had permitted this practice, the Company would have lost 200,000 *l.*

Caroor,

Caroor, on the borders of the Tritchinopoly country; Colonel Forbes with a ſtrong force, remained in the diſtricts of Daraporam and Dindigul; while Colonel Kelly, with another diviſion, advanced to Covanore on the borders of Madura and the Marawas. This diſtribution was intended to relieve your provinces from the burden of ſubſiſting too large a proportion of troops. At the ſame time the diviſions were ſo ſtationed, as to overawe every diſtrict to the ſouthward, and to form the army on the ſhorteſt notice, in the event of a renewal of the war againſt Tippoo Sultaun.

Having proceeded with the Cavanore diviſion, as the moſt central ſituation, to the ſouthward, theſe arrangements were hardly finiſhed* when I received your orders to reaſſemble the army, and to pre-

* On the twenty-fourth of January 1784.

pare

pare for a recommencement of hostility. You likewise directed me to retain possession of Palagatcherry, in case by any accident it should have been restored. I instantly issued orders to all the garrisons and stations to augment our equipment; wrote to Mr. Sulivan, Mr. Hippisley, and the other Gentlemen in the civil departments; intreating them to procure bullocks, gunney bags, and money for the pressing exigencies of the army: and farther made a circuit of the southern countries to accelerate these preparations. From Ramnad I went to Tinivelly to forward the business of money and conveyance, collecting for us there by Mr. Irwin; and from thence wrote to the Zamorin, exhorting him to retain Palagatcherry, which he had occupied after it was abandoned by Captain Wheeler. Captain Agnew was soon afterwards dispatched with a party of Sepoys, to solicit four battalions from the Rajah of Travancore, who very graciously complied with my my request; and by means of that assistance, Captain Agnew would no doubt have enabled the Zamorin to maintain the place, had not the Zamorin* and his adherents, despairing of support, abandoned the fort, and retired to their recesses in the mountains.

On the north-east border of the Tinivelly country, a letter reached me from the Commissioners, dated the eleventh of February near Mangalore, and written in terms which not only marked the enmity of Tippoo, but convinced me that a rupture was unavoidable; and this opinion was afterwards confirmed by a detail of particulars, in a letter from General Macleod. No time was therefore to be lost in ordering the stores to join Colonel Stuart's division near

* The Zamorin and his Followers of the Nyar cast are rigid Gentoos, and venerate the Bramins. Tippoo's soldiers, therefore, daily exposed the heads of many Bramins in sight of the fort. It is asserted that the Zamorin, rather than witness such enormities, chose to abandon Palagatcherry.

Caroor,

Caroor, and we marched the ſame night to Madura.

On my arrival at Covanore*, I found that fanams†, amounting to a lack of pagodas, had reached the camp from Tanjore. The impatience of the troops for this ſupply was proportioned to the ſeverity of their diſtreſs; excepting the prize-money at Palagatcherry, and the working money to the parties employed on extra labour, no ſums had been iſſued to the army during our whole progreſs, in croſſing and recroſſing India. Unfortunately the coin in which this payment was received, became a more copious ſource of diſcontent, than all the hardſhips they had endured. The ſtar pagoda‡ is underſtood to be the only legal tender of your Preſidency: it

* Colonel Kelly's diviſion was ſtationed there: it is on the confines of the Marawa country, leſs than twenty miles from Madura.

† Fanams are a ſmall coin of different value, compoſed of ſilver and copper.

‡ The ſtar pagoda is worth eight ſhillings.

is not coined to the ſouthward, but its place had uſually been ſupplied by the Porto Novo pagoda, which is leſs valuable by ten per cent. The Rajah of Tanjore has not exerciſed the right of coining pagodas, and of late has paid his tribute* in fanams. The Dutch coinage at Negapatam formerly amounted to four or five lacks of pagodas annually, but this has been diſcontinued ſince we got poſſeſſion of that city. As there is no gold coinage in any other place to the ſouthward, nor any regular circulation of rupees, the whole currency of thoſe provinces, exceeding the pagodas that happen to be in uſe, conſiſts of fanams; of theſe every diſtrict coins a different ſort, and no comparative rate having ever been eſtabliſhed between the ſtar pagodas and thoſe inferior coins, their value fluctuates according to the

* The tribute amounts to four lacks of pagodas, or 160,000*l.*

relative

relative demand, and the coinage of one province is seldom or never at par in another.

Whenever it is known that a large issuing of fanams is at hand, the Shroffs, Soucars, and Dubashes*, purchase all the pagodas they can procure. Thus the fanams are kept at a high price, till the disbursement has taken place, and the rate is fixed at the current exchange for the day. But no sooner has this fluctuating coin been circulated, than the pagodas come forth, and in forty-eight hours the holders of fanams suffer a depreciation of six, eight, or ten per cent. Still more oppressive is this medium of public payment, when the fanams are issued in a province to which they do not properly belong: for the Tanjore fanam has no regular currency in any

* Shroffs, Soucars, and Dubashes, are money changers, bankers, and black agents of the Europeans.

other

other province. And this applies to all coins of that description, fabricated in Tritchinopoly, Madura, Tinivelly, Ramnad, and Shevigunga.

The commercial evils from this debasement and diversity of coin are not less considerable. A merchant cannot make a remittance to any place north of the Coleroon, without much trouble and expence in purchasing pagodas, or else by an unreasonable premium to Soucars. The money remitted to the army from Tanjore was issued in Tanjore fanams, at the rate of twenty-two and an half per star pagoda: but when the Sepoys received this money in distant encampments, they found that twenty-four or twenty-five fanams were required for a pagoda there; nor could they in many instances, without enormous loss, procure the necessaries of life for those uncurrent fanams.

To

To prevent as much as poſſible the troops from ſuffering by a loſs upon exchange, which in common juſtice ſhould fall upon the public, it was propoſed to Mr. Sulivan, and immediately acceded to by him, that the paymaſter ſhould carry the difference to the account of the Company. It was therefore directed, that the officers commanding diviſions of the army, ſhould form a Board to aſcertain the loſs ſuſtained by each battalion, and Mr. Digby, paymaſter in camp, was inſtructed to give credit to the corps for the amount of loſs incurred, agreeably to the general ſtatement tranſmitted to me by the abovementioned Board.

It appeared requiſite to be minute in this recapitulation, in order to impreſs the neceſſity of reform in the ſouthern payments. This will be effected, by ordering a large coinage of pagodas, and by eſtabliſhing a tarif or proportional value between the pagodas and fanams, in the ſame manner as in in England twenty-one ſhillings are at all times equivalent to a guinea.

My next object was to concert meaſures with Mr. Sulivan for the ſafety of the ſouthern countries, while the army ſhould, for the third time, advance into the enemy's dominions. With this view I proceeded to Tanjore, and from thence by Tritchinopoly joined the main diviſion at Caroor. You had been pleaſed to reinforce us from the Preſidency with the ninety-eighth regiment, a party of European artillerymen, and ſome heavy ordnance. Other guns were received from Tanjore, and the exertions of Mr. Sulivan procured us many articles in which we had been before deficient.

During my late progreſs through the ſouthern countries, Mr. Digby called forth every exertion of his perſonal credit, and in addition to conveyance for the whole ordnance, ammunition, and ſtores of the army, he had actually provided carriage complete for 300,000 fears of rice; which at the rate of one fear per day for 15,000 men, amounted to twenty days provifion, exclufive of other conveyance, amounting to ten days more. The main body of the army was affembled at Caroor, excepting the divifion with Colonel Forbes, which remained in force at Daraporam, ready to join at the fhorteft notice. Nothing farther was wanting but fpecific orders from your Lordfhip and the Board, or from the Commiffioners, to re-commence hoftility; and I had ftill a plan of operations in view, that promifed to lead us to the capital of Myfore by a route not lefs favourable than that which we had been directed to relinquifh, in cafe it fhould have been judged neceffary to renew the war. This event became extremely probable from the recent conduct of our adverfaries. Previoufly to my arrival at Caroor a foraging party had been attacked, and an European officer, who fell into the enemy's hands,

hands, was closely confined at Sankarydurgum. The second battalion had been advanced from General Jones's force to the northward, and was entirely cut to pieces by Tippoo's troops near Cumalum; while Tippoo himself, finding that the southern army was ordered to abandon his country, and that no other force could venture to oppose him, persisted in his investment of Mangalore, and compelled that distinguished garrison to yield at last to the necessity of famine, and surrender the place*.

Notwithstanding the flagrant treachery by which Mangalore was lost, and the deliberate massacre of General Mathews, with many other captive English officers, the treaty of peace was mutually signed on the eleventh of February, and exchanged between the Commissioners and Tippoo Sultaun.

* Colonel Campbell marched off with his few remaining troops to Telicherry, agreeably to the stipulation with Tippoo, and died soon after, worn out with fatigue.

taun*. The treaty ſpecified the enlargement of the Buſhwanna or Amuldar of Palagatcherry, whom we had detained in order to give evidence concerning the murder of a party of Europeans taken priſoners near Palagat, at the time that Colonel Humberſtone's army was before that place †. He was ſent with an eſcort to the camp of Nawas Begg, and from thence returned me his thanks for the good treatment he experienced. This was the only ſubject of Tip-

* As I have ſtated at ſome length the circumſtances that led me to conſider a continuation of the war as eligible, it might be expected that I ſhould alſo have explained the many and perhaps unanſwerable arguments that induced the government of Madras to adopt a contrary conduct. In addreſſing that Board, an enumeration of thoſe arguments would have been ſuperfluous and impertinent; but it would be an injuſtice to the merit of their determination, if I omitted here to remark, that the tenor of inſtructions from home, the ſtate of negociations in Europe and the impoveriſhed condition of the Company's territories, concurred to impreſs the ableſt men in India with the propriety and neceſſity of that meaſure, which procured to Lord Macartney's Government the warmeſt acknowledgments and approbation of their ſuperiors.

† This party was put to death by the expreſs order of Tippoo Sultaun.

poo

poo who had not been immediately released, although nearly 10,000 prisoners had been taken by us during the operations of the southern army. The Commissioners also directed me to restore the forts and countries of Caroor and Daraporam, but to retain possession of Dindigul, and to station a strong force there until the English prisoners should be actually enlarged.

No time was lost in evacuating the specified countries; and on the first of April Colonel Forbes's division moved to Dindigul, and Colonel Stuart fell back from Caroor upon the province of Tritchinopoly, with instructions to deposit all the stores and heavy ordnance of the army in that garrison. While we remained at Dindigul, the troops in that quarter suffered a continuation of fatigue, and were obliged to march seventy miles to the head of the Oultumpollum valley, to receive the grain necessary for their current subsistence.

 In

In obedience to your orders defiring my opinion on the moft advantageous mode of reforming and arranging the fouthern forces, I had the honour, on the twenty-fixth of April, to exprefs my fentiments on that important fubject*, and ftated that the vicinity of Tritchinopoly was the moft eligible pofition for a cantonment, where a ftrong force, complete in every circumftance of field equipment, fhould at all times be ftationed;—that the great depofit of military ftores and provifions fhould be formed there, with the field and battering train, pioneers, and main body of the fouthern artillery;—that the Commandants of corps fhould be charged with the carriage of their battalion-tents, ftores, and ammunition, as well as rice, if requifite, at the ufual rates fpecified in the Company's regulations. It was alfo fuggefted, that whenever military aid fhould be found neceffary

* See that Letter in the Appendix.

for

for the interior buſineſs of the country, the civil Chiefs, Reſidents, and Superintendants ſhould addreſs their applications, not to the ſubordinate officers caſually employed in the different diſtricts, but to the Southern Commander, in order that the requiſition might be complied with from the main ſtation or cantonment of the ſouthern forces. By theſe means the troops would be preſerved in a conſtant ſtate of diſcipline, the jarrings incident to the detail of ſubordinate interference between civil and military would be avoided, and every corps would have a rotation of detachment duty. An immediate reduction of Peons, Tynauts, and other irregulars, was alſo recommended, to the amount of 10,000 men; from whence a monthly ſaving of 25 or 30,000 pagodas would ariſe. I flattered myſelf, that the adoption of arrangements propoſed in that letter would have removed the deficiencies under which the ſouthern forces labour; and that, in the event of

 hoſtility

hoſtility in that part of India, they would have added ſuch vigour to your operations as would have precluded a renewal of thoſe calamities which occurred during the Carnatic war.

By the end of May, it became impracticable to ſubſiſt ſo large a force in the Dindigul country. A ſtrong garriſon was therefore left in that fortreſs, and the diviſion was withdrawn towards Madura, where the Europeans and ſome native corps were cantoned. As ſoon as the review of the battalions was finiſhed, which had engaged me for ſeveral months, three battalions were detached under Captain Wheeler to the Tinivelly country; and, at the ſame time, it became neceſſary for me to move thither in perſon in order to arrange a permanency of payment and ſupply for the troops in that province. Some occurrences which happened there reſpecting the Polygars, Catabominaigue, and Shevigherry, were immediately

diately communicated to your President; and evinced the refractory disposition of that race. From Tinivelly I proceeded by Negapatam and Tanjore to Tritchinopoly, in order to provide by personal endeavours for the distresses of the troops.

It now remained for me to undergo a duty more painful than all the embarrassments hitherto experienced. Your Lordship and the Board found it requisite to order a reduction of many thousand independents, and other southern irregulars, who had been raised by his Highness the Nabob Mahomed Ally. During the whole period of misfortunes to the southward, they still bore the rigour of distress with a resignation unknown to Europeans. Among these men, there were the most respectable soldiers of the east; some of them had followed their fathers into the Carnatic, in the days of Doost Ally, and Anwaradeen Cawn; others had remained in the

the ſervice ſince the days of Chunda Saheb, and the depoſed Rana or Gentoo queen of Tritchinopoly. Many of them had continued ſince the campaigns of Lawrence, Clive, and Iſoof Cawn, in a conſtant ſeries of military duty. To theſe wretched adherents, an average of twelve months pay was due. The misfortunes of the times rendered it impoſſible to diſcharge thoſe claims, for the regular corps of the army were not leſs in arrears: under ſuch circumſtances, to turn them looſe to miſery, while the country was in a ſtate that could afford them no relief, would have diſtreſſed the moſt unfeeling mind. They aſſailed me daily with their ſufferings, and the only expedient was adopted, that promiſed to combine the duties of obedience with the obligations of humanity, by directing the officers commanding the corps of thoſe irregulars, to furniſh me with rolls, containing the names of each black officer and Sepoy under their command, ſpecifying

ing the length of ſervice, and arrears of pay; in order that each of them might receive a certificate of his demand on the Company, to be counterſigned by the officer, and by the commandant of the garriſon with which the corps correſponded; and at the ſame time deſiring a particular recommendation of every individual who had any pretenſion to indulgence.

This being finiſhed, our, next object was, to diſband the raw and undeſerving rabble, who had been collected during the diſtracted period of the ſouthern affairs. They were ordered to receive on the firſt of each ſucceeding month, thirty days ſubſiſtence in grain, until their arrears ſhould be diſcharged. The ancient and reſpectable part of thoſe corps, were to be continued on the rolls, until we ſhould be able to procure ſome adequate proviſion for ſo deſerving a claſs of public ſervants. In neither inſtance however, did

did my endeavours prove effectual. The latter clafs of venerable veterans remains unprovided for; and the monthly iffuing of grain depending on your renters and civil fervants, it was not within the limits of my power to enforce performance. So much was it neglected by the renter of Tritchinopoly, that after my departure from the fouthward, thefe unfortunate victims, impelled by hunger, were driven to fuch excefs in their endeavours to procure relief, as obliged the military commandant to reprefs them by force of arms.

To thefe painful incidents were added, the claims and diftreffes of the army encamped near Tritchinopoly. The troops were accuftomed to endure twelve or fourteen months arrears with unexampled forbearance, and the public followers, attendants on the army, had long been ftrangers to any coin; when to this was added, a failure of their daily allowance of grain

grain in lieu of batta, their caſe would have been truly deſperate, had not Tondiman advanced a month's proviſion for their relief. Such were the abuſes of the renter at Tritchinopoly, that in a favourable ſeaſon the place was menaced by famine. His diſinclination to have a diviſion ſtationed in the diſtrict, ſuggeſted ſo ſtrange a mode of effecting their removal. But by this machination any troops leſs patient than ours would have been excited to revolt; and the fort of Tritchinopoly would have fallen to Tippoo, if he had thought proper to inveſt it at the moment.

So urgent was our diſtreſs that I found myſelf obliged, without any previous communication, to diſperſe the troops in queſt of ſubſiſtence; the 78th to Tanjore, the Hanoverians towards Tripatore, a large body of Sepoys towards Madura, and other battalions to Mellore and the Marawas.— At the ſame time the 101ſt, and ſoon after the

the 98th, were ordered to the Preſidency, to embark from thence for Bengal in their way to Europe.

Your Lordſhip and the Board were fully impreſſed with the neceſſity of reducing the public followers and field eſtabliſhment of the army, in order to lighten the burden of expenditure, and to liquidate part of thoſe arrears already incurred; but the protraction of the treaty with Tippoo unavoidably induced you to defer that meaſure, until the mutual reſtitution of Amboor and Dindigul ſhould be effected. That event at laſt took place, while his cruel maſſacre was ſtrong in every memory, while his inſulting treatment of thoſe whom he releaſed excited general indignation, and while his detention of 200 * Engliſh

* He had made them be circumciſed and enrolled in his ſervice.

prisoners

prisoners seemed to preclude all pacific expectations *.

I hastened to Fort St. George, to lay before your Right Honourable President, a faithful statement of your southern affairs; of our proceedings and expenditure; as well as to explain the meritorious conduct of the troops in that quarter, and the eminent exertions made by Mr. Sulivan and Mr. Irwin at the head of the civil departments; to prove that even their abilities had not been able entirely to correct the evils hitherto inherent in the southern system; and to point out resources for the speedy liquidation of the army arrears; it was my inten-

* I must again be permitted to remark, that such were the embarrassments and distress under which the different Presidencies laboured, that, notwithstanding these incidents, the treaty of peace with Tippoo Sultaun was generally considered as a measure eligible for the English interests in India: It is also a prevalent opinion, that if the negotiations had not been conducted under some unfavourable circumstances, the distinguished knowledge and abilities of Sir George Staunton were peculiarly adapted to procure the most beneficial terms.

intention from thence to have embarked with my own regiment for Bengal, where I ſhould have been ſenior officer of the King's ſervice, and ſecond in command on that eſtabliſhment; but I could not think of withdrawing from the ſouthern ſtation while any thing remained for me to re-preſent in behalf of your ſouthern forces.

Permit me now, My Lord and Gentlemen, to offer my beſt apologies for the tediouſneſs of this recapitulation.—It exhibits various incidents, in their riſe, progreſs, and completion. In this view, it may prove not altogether unintereſting to that claſs of public ſervants who wiſh to derive after-information from paſt tranſactions.—At all events, I preſume, it has ſufficiently evinced that our endeavours having proved leſs permanently advantageous than might have been expected, aroſe from the circumſtances under which we acted, and can

can neither be attributed to me, nor to the army I commanded.

It is fully known to your Board, that the ſyſtem of conciliation to which Mr. Sulivan and myſelf had rigidly adhered *, does not accord with the opinions of any conſiderable portion of either ſervice. Various circumſtances of contention had for many years excited enmity between the civil and military.—Theſe habits of diſunion were greatly ſtrengthened during the government of Sir Thomas Rumbold, when the pretenſions of your ſubordinate Chiefs were either eſtabliſhed or confirmed. By the regulations alluded to, the commandant of a garriſon or province came under the detail command of the civil Chief. The Chief received reports and paroles, kept the

* Notwithſtanding the diſſenſions that raged among all ranks of Europeans in India, I had the good fortune to avoid every ſpecies of diſcuſſion; having neither exhibited a charge, nor been the ſubject of complaint from any perſon in the country.

keys of the garriſon, and had direction of ſtores, magazines, and defences in the fort. Hence it happened during the late war, that the command was not delegated to the military officer until the enemy were in motion againſt the place. Then it was only ſo delegated, that the Chief might provide for his own ſafety, and throw the odium of ſurrender on the Commander. Thus, inſtead of a regular military control, a ſyſtematic animoſity prevailed: the magazines were left without grain, the garriſons without ſtores, and the country ſo deſtitute of preparation*, that on the irruption of Hyder Ally, the forts in the Carnatic fell an eaſy prey to the invader. Theſe irritations were too frequently increaſed by military vehemence on the one hand, and by aſſumptions of the civil ſervice on the other.

As the natives of Indoſtan have little reſpect for any but the military character,

* Before the commencement of the war, the forts throughout the Carnatic were in general under the orders of the Nabob's government.

the

the civil ſervants, in order to acquire conſequence, have uſually aſſumed a ſuperiority over the military. Thus the Chief or Reſident was frequently held forth as the Phouzdar or General of the province, who was prevented by greater objects from taking the field, but whoſe mandates the ſoldiery were bound to obey. The recent conteſts between Government and the military Commanders, together with the unuſual proportion of king's officers lately employed in India, have unavoidably thrown into circulation a greater maſs of opinions adverſe to the civil ſervice, and given a greater currency to military pretenſions, than could be expected from the officers of your own eſtabliſhment: to theſe irritating circumſtances has been added, the extreme preſſure of perſonal diſtreſs in a pernicious climate, where there is perpetual hoſtility and continued fatigue.

During the late war, many officers were obliged to ſell their furniture and wearing apparel, in order to procure a ſcanty ſubſiſtence; while others could not poſſibly find means of appearing as became their ſtation. If a pittance of their arrears was to be advanced, it often came attended with circumſtances ſo ſingularly diſreputable, that nothing ſhort of penury could juſtify the offer or acceptance; if in Company's bonds, they were hardly negotiable; if in Bengal bills, the holders of them loſt thirty, forty, or fifty per cent; and if the payment took place in an out-garriſon, the diſcretion or caprice of the paymaſter alone determined the mode of payment. Needy officers, at the mercy of ſuch a ſuperior, have frequently ſubmitted to receive a month's arrears in rice, teas, wines, and other merchandize*. When theſe and ſimilar incidents

* The diſtreſſes of the country, the want of money, and the calamities of war, rendered it impracticable for the Board

dents recur to your remembrance; when you recollect how patiently your troops have ſuffered, and how bravely they have fought; you will undoubtedly admit, that their preſent diſcontents are not ill founded, and that their grievances call loudly for redreſs.

It is by the good order and efficiency of the military conſtitution alone, that the Engliſh dominions in the Eaſt can be preſerved. This is requiſite, not merely to repel invaſion, but for the current buſineſs of your poſſeſſions, which you have never yet been able to conduct without military power. If therefore, an habitual intervention of the military in detail of civil management, juſtifies the appellation of military government, there is no country

Board of Madras to prevent theſe evils; on the contrary, the important operations effected by that Government, under the preſſure of ſuch embarraſſments, is one of the ſtrongeſt teſtimonies that can be adduced in proof of their talents, fortitude, and exertion.

 on

on earth ſo peculiarly entitled to that deſignation as the Engliſh ſettlements in India. Beſides, as no country can be more habituated to convulſions, wars, and revolutions, it follows that the public endeavours ſhould be ſtrenuouſly directed to obtain perfection in the military ſyſtem.

When we compare the diſcipline of your troops, and the conſtitution of your armies, with thoſe of other European powers in India, the ſuperiority is evidently with the Engliſh; but when we look back to the days of Clive and Lawrence, to the ſmallneſs of their force, and the magnitude of their atchievements, we muſt confeſs that more recent occurrences have exhibited a mortifying contraſt. The hiſtory of many years preceding the period of your Government, is filled with the detail of our impolicy. The beſt regiments of cavalry upon the Coaſt were driven from the Nabob's ſervice to the enemy. Garriſons were

were left deſtitute of military ſtores, or proviſion: ſhameful aggreſſions* were committed againſt every native power: unjuſt wars were unſkilfully conducted: there were neither preparations, concert, nor precaution: forts fell at the firſt ſummons, detachments were cut off, armies were captured, countries depopulated, a ruinous conteſt† was concluded by a degrading pacification, only to make way for ſtill more humiliating events; the troops were ſtarving, the treaſury empty, all credit gone, and all ranks diſſatisfied. The empire of opinion, which we had obtained in India, was thrown away; and there remained a manifeſt impoſſibility of maintaining the territorial empire in its waſted and diſtracted condition.

Theſe form but an incomplete enumeration of circumſtances that mark the haſty progreſs of our decline. The Arabs have

* No faith in our treaties.

† War of 1767 with Hyder.

fallen, the Moors have degenerated, the Portugueſe have decayed, the Dutch have dwindled, the French are bereft of territory: all of them have been great and powerful, and conquerors in India; all of them have paid the forfeit of miſconduct. The Engliſh having attained a loftineſs of ſituation in the Eaſt beyond the moſt aſpiring fancy of their rivals, are now precipitating from their elevation; and thus they are leaving a monitory example to all future innovators, that no energy of former atchievement or extent of actual power can ſupport a Government while waſting with internal principles of diſſolution.

If we are to look for a renovation of the Engliſh intereſts in India, it muſt ariſe from ſuch exertions as thoſe of your Right Honourable Preſident. The difficulties with which you have ſucceſsfully contended, the counteraction you have experienced, and your ability under moſt perplexing circumſtances,

ſtances, yield a well-grounded expectation, that in the proſecution of a general and digeſted reform, your labours would be crowned with the utmoſt brilliancy of ſucceſs.

Of all the objects within your Preſidency, the improvement of your military ſyſtem is the moſt urgent and the leaſt difficult. The diſcipline and manœuvres of the European and Sepoy infantry, as well as of your artillery and the few cavalry in your ſervice, are formed on the beſt models of Europe; and it is aſſerted that, before the war, their appearance would have done credit to any ſervice, while their gallantry and endurance form a ſubject of hiſtorical applauſe.

The officers upon the coaſt are habituated to act in emergencies with a facility that few ſubordinate officers in Europe ever

have

have a profpect of acquiring. Before an officer attains the rank of Captain, he muft unavoidably have been often charged with the command of parties on diftant marches, in the conveyance of ftores, in the guard of pofts and ftrongholds, in the bufinefs of collection, and in menacing of refractory Polygars, together with every other feries of duty which can occur. From hence it will be found, that there are few fervices indeed where fo many men poffefs the practical requifites of an officer. How ftrongly have zeal, knowledge, and ability been exemplified during the late conteft, by thofe who command your Sepoy battalions?—With what addrefs did they foothe the fufferings of their foldiers, relieve their wants, and reftrain the well-grounded clamours of men, whom the public neceffities had left in extremity of diftrefs! Thefe confiderations fuggeft the benefit of reftraining indifcriminate admiffion into the fervice, ſervice, and of ſelecting a ſucceſſion of deſerving officers for the command of all your corps.

The higher orders of your ſervice, no doubt, poſſeſs in a ſtill ſtronger degree the practical advantages now deſcribed; but as the military riſe in India is by rotation without purchaſe, it is ſcarcely poſſible to become a field officer in leſs than twenty years. Few conſtitutions are equal, in that climate, to ſo long a ſeries of fatigue. Beſides, your field officers in general command the conſiderable garriſons. As they regimentally belong to the four battalions of your two regiments of European infantry, theſe corps are frequently left to the junior Captains, who are ſolicitous of procuring appointments to the Sepoys, and take little intereſt in the diſcipline of the Europeans. But may not the command of an European corps be rendered permanent and advantageous, like thoſe in England?

May

May not the condition of ancient officers be relieved by the eſtabliſhment of half-pay, and the permiſſion of ſelling their commiſſions? By theſe means, thoſe who are diſqualified for zealous execution of their duty, might retire with a proviſion for their after-days, and give opportunities of advancement to others more earneſt in purſuit of military reputation.

The growing ſtrength and diſcipline of your enemies, and our late diſaſters, point out the wiſdom of Sir Eyre Coote's requiſitions for an increaſe of Europeans to form the central ſtrength of your armies. He maintained that at leaſt 10,000 Europeans ſhould be conſtantly complete for ſervice in the three Preſidencies. An objection has ariſen from the quick mortality occaſioning a burdenſome demand for new ſupplies of men; but this may be in a great meaſure remedied, by ſalutary preparations for the reception of the recruits from Europe,—by ſtationing

ſtationing them in healthy quarters, enforcing regularity, and reſtraining the ſale of arrack and other pernicious liquors.

With regard to your Sepoys, the public ſhould be watchful of their diſcipline, and liberal to confirm their attachment. It is by their good conduct that your ſettlements have hitherto been preſerved, and to them you are to truſt for after-ſtability. That they are partial to your ſervice, is evinced by recent experience. Let them receive the common juſtice due to every ſoldier; let them be regularly paid and enabled to ſubſiſt their families;—let the wiſe inſtitution of admitting the children of wounded or deſerving Sepoys, to be enrolled and to draw pay from the battalions, be continued; and the Black officers be treated with indulgence and reſpect. It is farther requiſite that the mode of iſſuing pay be ſo amended as to remove any poſſible imputation of fraudulent exactions committed againſt

against the Sepoys, by usurious advances of money in the moments of distress, by undue stoppages for articles which either have not been furnished or are overcharged, and by other unjustifiable practices. In that case we may venture to pronounce, that while their expertness in manœuvre, the interior œconomy of the battalions, and the conduct of their officers, continue to inspire them with a sense of superiority, no probable events can shake their adherence. As the European officers on the Coast are not generally conversant with the country languages, it may be farther proper to direct, that every one aspiring to the command or adjutancy of a Sepoy corps, should first learn the Moorish or Malabar dialect.

Although I cannot persuade myself, that it is judicious to admit Parias * into battalions with men of reputable casts †; yet

* Parias are the outcasts of the country, and are held to be impure by the Gentoos.

† Casts mean the different classes or sects to which Gentoos belong.

 assuredly

aſſuredly the mixture of Moormen, Rajahpoots, Gentoos, and Malabars in the ſame corps, is extremely beneficial, for it ſtimulates by emulation, and reſtrains all dangerous confederacies, which cannot eſcape the jealouſy of contending ſects. I have alſo recommended the corps of Topaſſees or deſcendants of Europeans, who retain the characteriſtic qualities of their progenitors. They form a check upon the other native troops, and are more eaſily maintained in movements of difficulty; for they eat any food like Europeans, and that corps would alſo become a nurſery for hundreds of children who are yearly loſt to the community.

The expences attending your cavalry have deprived you of that eſſential conſtituent of an army. Indeed, the ſtrange impolicy which drove four well-appointed regiments from the Nabob's ſervice to that of Hyder, has left you with ſcarcely a

ſuffi-

ſufficiency of horſe to form a grand guard in front of your main army.—All parties admit the neceſſity of augmenting that branch of your eſtabliſhment; eſpecially as your enemy * can bring more than 60,000 horſemen into the field. But the extravagant rates at which your troop horſes are purchaſed, the ſtill more extravagant price at which they are maintained, the unreaſonable pay of your troopers, and the laviſh allowances to cavalry officers, render it almoſt chimerical to ſuggeſt the means of new modelling that ſervice.

Notwithſtanding theſe objections, a plan had occurred to me, which, if it had been my lot to remain in India, ſhould have been ſubmitted to your conſideration, for raiſing 5,000 horſe at a moderate rate.—The troopers to receive only a ſmall proportion of pay more than the infantry, and

* Tippoo Sultaun. The Marattas can bring 100,000, and the Nizam 60,000 horſe into the field.

the

the horses to be fed at a very reduced allowance, without any farther contract, contingency, or extra charge.—Thus the expence of a cavalry establishment would be brought within the limits of the Coast finances. Neither would any engagements on the part of Government be required, except that the officer charged with the execution should be established in one of the great northern stations, and that the Nizam, as well as other country Powers, should admit his agents to purchase horses freely throughout their territories. Lastly, that Government should order all renters and collectors of revenue in the possessions of the Company and of the Nabob not to charge more than eight shillings, or one pagoda *per* 100 measures, for all the gram* furnished to the cavalry, which, at the rate of one pagoda *per* month, would be an allowance to each horse of more than three measures *per* day.

* A kind of pulse on which horses are fed in India.

The artillery has become a great inſtrument of military operations in the ſyſtem of Indian warfare, and has maintained a reputation hardly ſurpaſſed in any ſervice. It may not however be unneceſſary to obſerve, that the augmentation of ſo ponderous a machinery is attended with unſupportable expence, and obſtructs thoſe ſudden and unexpected movements by which the great events in India have been atchieved. But whether it is to be continued on an extended or contracted ſcale, the department of ſtores, artificers, and conveyance, forming the great appendage of the artillery, calls aloud for reformation.

It has already been ſuggeſted, that all the corps ought to be equipped with a ſufficiency of artificers and conveyance for the repairs and movements of their own baggage, ſtores, and ammunition. Thus they will be at all times ready for emergencies, and the ſtore department will be re-

lieved

lieved from the embarraſſment of carrying muſket ammunition, with which it is at preſent encumbered, as well as with various other articles belonging to the battalions.

The numerous body of Laſcars, artificers, and other public followers attached to that department, conſtitute the next object of conſideration. They ſhould aſſuredly be regimented, or formed into corps under the command of European officers, reſponſible for their conduct, proficiency, and regular receipt of pay. From the want of ſuch an arrangement during the late diſtreſſes, all regular diſburſements to the troops were impeded, and the public followers were often ſhamefully neglected. Much benefit would alſo be derived from ſeparating the complement belonging to the field and battering train; and from eſtabliſhing in each cantonment a commiſſary of ſtores, provided with every article neceſſary to enable the diviſion to which he belongs,

 to

to move on the ſhorteſt notice, without reference to the ſtore-keepers of garriſons, who are not ſufficiently under military control to be entruſted with military preparation.

It is farther extremely requiſite, that your corps of Pioneers ſhould be encreaſed, not only for the ſake of expertneſs and diſpatch in the preparations of a ſiege, but to facilitate the rapid movements of your armies. So attentive was Hyder to this branch of his eſtabliſhment, that he ſeldom maintained fewer than 5,000 Commooty men, or Pioneers, who preceded his line, cleared the roads, and enabled him to move with a celerity ſeldom equalled by Europeans.

The abuſes* and deficiencies in your bullock department, have long been the ſubject of complaint. When Sir Eyre

* The great maſs of army conveyance in India, is performed by bullocks.

Coote in 1782 required 30,000 bullocks, to enable the Carnatic army to move with effect, the total number actually serving with it did not, I believe, exceed 9,000; nor has that army ever been able to procure a complement for distant operations. To this cause has been chiefly attributed the failure of the Carnatic war, and indeed the evil in question seems almost beyond a remedy; for the principal black men, who used to engage their bullocks* in your service, have been suffered to run muster upon muster in arrears, after spending their stock, and straining their credit on the public faith: and at last, such have been the distresses of the times, with more than twelve months of unliquidated balance due to them, and after having lost many hundreds of their cattle through fatigue and sickness, they

* The rate at which bullocks are hired for the public service is two and a half pagodas per month for a draught bullock, and two pagodas for a carriage bullock. The southern army hired them for less by a half pagoda per month, or twenty-five per cent.

 have

have been diſmiſſed from the Company's employment.

It was not by ſuch means that the Engliſh character became reſpectable in this country. There was a period no farther diſtant than the days of General Lawrence, when the natives of Indoſtan held the engagements of an Engliſhman to be unalterable; they repreſented him with all the attributes of prroweſs in war, and of juſtice in peace. Thus confidence and veneration were ſo mingled in their eſtimation of him, that their ſenſations of ſecurity were ſtronger under an Engliſh authority, than under the beſt of their native princes. In thoſe days the purſe of the individual was ever open to the public exigency, for every individual confided in the faith and credit of the public. It muſt be confeſſed that a ſtrict adherence to engagement, and the ſanctity of public faith, were never more conſpicuous than under your Government, but

but unfortunately the miſconduct of your predeceſſors left you deſtitute of means to maintain that promptitude of diſburſement, and liberality of reward, by which the Engliſh firſt roſe to elevation in India.*

The next material object is, the department of Engineers, including not only preparations for beſieging, but the defenſive condition of your forts. You have a reſpectable corps of Engineers, under an officer diſtinguiſhed for his talents of arrangement. An official enquiry into the actual ſtate and deficiencies of proviſions, ammunition, and other military ſtores, would enable you to aſcertain the ſpecific complement that ſhould at all times be preſerved in every garriſon of Coromandel.

The inſpection and deſcriptive report of all the ſouthern garriſons, which are the moſt important on your Coaſt, have long ago been completed; for, as ſoon as the army returned from the enemy's country, Captain Byres* was requested by me to undertake a survey of Tanjore, Tritchinopoly, Madura, Pallamcottah, and Ramnad. This he executed with the utmost ability, and also transmitted to your Presidency a statement of every particular respecting those garrisons, expressed in accurate and comprehensive terms; there remains little farther therefore, except to bestow a similar attention on the other forts, and above all, most rigidly to enforce obedience to such orders, for replenishing the magazines, and augmenting the complement of stores, as your Engineers and a Committee of Inspection may suggest. But vain will these measures prove, unless the stores, magazines, and fortifications, be subjected to severe and periodical examinations, and unless the Commandant of the place be enabled to enforce your instructions. On the other hand, if the military store-keepers and civil managers

* Chief Engineer to the southward.

be

be suffered to disregard all orders of the Commandant, in the direction of the magazines, and preparations for defence, assuredly the responsibility in moments of attack should likewise be transferred to them, that there might be some restraint, at least, on their negligence or indiscretion.

The late degrading scenes of surrender without resistance at Arcot, Cuddelore, Permacoil, and almost at every other place* where the enemy made any vigorous attack, have suggested an œconomical expedient of destroying many inferior garrisons throughout the country. But your Board will recollect, that every thing was venal on the Coast for years before Hyder ventured an invasion;—that he had secretly purchased the Killidarships † of Arnee, Gingee, Carnatic Gur, Thiagar, and various other posts of strength. These he filled with emissaries of his own, who, on

* Vellore and Wandivash were the only exceptions.

† Killidar is the Moorish Commandant of a place.

his

his first approach, secured the European officer, if there was one, and surrendered: for those important places were entirely garrisoned by undisciplined dependents of the Nabob. But unless these or similar posts are re-occupied, filled with supplies, and defended by regulars, there can be no security of communication and subsistence; much less can offensive measures be effected from the Carnatic into the enemy's country. It will farther be found almost impracticable to repeople the Carnatic, without forts and strong holds; for the inhabitants fly from situations that afford not protection against predatory cavalry*.

Besides replenishing these inferior forts, the country cannot be secure without better regulation in your considerable garrisons,

* On this question it is but justice to remark that the best military opinions are divided; and at any rate there is little doubt, that if there were a respectable body of cavalry on the Coast establishment, the necessity of maintaining the inferior forts would in a great measure cease.

and

and a diſtribution of your remaining force into three great frontier cantonments. The main or central one in the Carnatic, ſomewhere between Arcot and Vellore; the ſecond, or ſouthern one, near Tritchinopoly; and the third at Ellore, or in ſome other northern poſition. The laſt would enable you to act in defence of the Circars, in conjunction with the Nizam, or againſt Tippoo's northern poſſeſſions of Cudapah and Kanoul, as circumſtances might require. Were the main body of your forces thus eſtabliſhed in a connected range upon the enemy's frontiers, the movements of the Carnatic army would no longer continue circumſcribed and inefficient as they have been; neither would Tippoo dare to penetrate into your poſſeſſions, leſt you ſhould retaliate with ſuperior facility againſt his own.

But we cannot expect a permanency of arrangement in the preſent indefinite ſtate of of military command:—while the power that ſhould direct and the power that ſhould obey are at variance, while the ſubordinates are at the mercy of contradictory orders from contending authorities,—nothing but counteraction can enſue. The inferior officer looks not to his commander for preferment, nor cares for his diſpleaſure, provided his acquieſcence with the civil intereſt can procure him an appointment. The condition of the Commander is ſtill more humiliating:—without weight to reſiſt the encroachments of the civil ſervice, his oppoſition only expoſes his weakneſs, and his compliance infallibly forfeits the confidence of the army:—involved in odious diſcuſſions, and being overwhelmed with committee buſineſs, a very ſmall portion of his thoughts is beſtowed upon the duties of his ſtation. Hence, for years paſt, there have been no regular reviews, no inſpection of the troops on the part of the Commander in chief,—no enforcement of the

eſtabliſhed

established regulations of the Coast service, and so little encouragement of parade duty, that the discipline of the army depends solely at this time on the meritorious attention of subordinate officers.

There appears but one remedy for these inveterate evils. While the power of a Governor rests upon a different basis from that of a Commander in chief, the passion for superiority will occasion violent and dangerous collision. The mass of the civil service espouse the cause of their Governor; the body of the army range under the banners of their General. The first are able and united;—the others are superior in vehemence and number. The discontented of the civil service make common cause with the military;—the obsequious of the military take shelter under the wing of civil patronage. Hence a general ferment is excited:——The civil service prosecute their measures with methodical assiduity;—the

the military indulge in clamorous excess. The grounds of discontent are communicated to the numerous attendants who surround all Europeans:—from these they spread through other classes of the natives, and extending over the peninsula involve every Englishman in the hatred and contempt of all India. The Asiatics cannot enter into European distinctions of participated power:—while they behold Generals seizing Governors, and Governors arresting Generals, they necessarily think ill of either situation.

So indispensable in all Eastern Government is power undisputed and control without counteraction, that we cannot hope to see a period put to these calamities until authority shall issue from one source, and flow in one equal undivided stream. Were this the case,—were the powers of Governor and Commander in chief united in the same person, still subjecting all public acts of Govern-

Government to the voice of a council or committee, the civil and military would forget their animofities; and inftead of regarding each other as contending fquadrons, they would feel themfelves confederate forces acting under the fame leader. No longer would the deliberative plans for the conduct of a war be thwarted by reluctant execution or actual difobedience, nor the moft alluring hopes of decifive enterprife be ftifled by the fparing hand that fhould fupport them. Neither can it be conceived, that from this amendment any difadvantage would refult to the military. At prefent they have the mortification to behold their leader without power, influence, or refpect: in the other cafe, he would poffefs them all. Were the fame perfon Governor and Commander in chief, the officer next in feniority would naturally be entrufted with the general conduct of the army, and enjoy confideration due to the fecond in command

command of a great military eſtabliſhment. Thus the ungovernable feuds of party would be checked, and there would be ſome proſpect that the public welfare might engage the undiſtracted attention of thoſe to whom it was entruſted.

With regard to your civil ſervice, it poſſeſſes many advantages. The young gentlemen ſent out in that capacity are, in general, well educated; and on their arrival at the Preſidency, are admitted to aſſiſt in the buſineſs of the different offices, including nearly the whole detail of public proceedings that can occur in any government. In fact, ſuch has been the ſalutary operation of theſe initiations, that your Preſidency alone has produced more men of extended capacity in buſineſs, than could probably be found in all the public offices of London. Theſe acquirements are extended, as the individual advances in the ſervice. He is ſucceſſively employed

as

as Paymaſter and Store-keeper of a garriſon, Paymaſter and Commiſſary of an army, Reſident with a country prince, Superintendant and Collector of a province, or Chief of a ſubordinate ſettlement in the regular gradation towards Council and Committee. In each of theſe employments, the current tranſactions are more weighty, the reſponſibility more immediately perſonal, and the duty more comprehenſive than uſually fall to the lot of any unexalted individual in England. It is in your power to direct towards important public purpoſes thoſe uſeful qualifications, and to do away any exiſting imperfections.

Once more allow me to repeat the aſſertion, that no ſervant in the civil department, entruſted with the charge of military ſtores in a garriſon, nor any one holding an appointment with an army, ſhould be ſuffered to conſider himſelf as independent of the Commandant. While ſanction is given to ſo unwarrantable an aſſumption, nothing but negligence and diſcord can take place. For experience aſcertains, that the main contentions in India have ariſen from the colliſion of interfering pretenſions. Theſe cannot exiſt, where the mutual relations of obedience and command are accurately defined. Every officer obeys, with ſatisfaction, the orders of your Board as the ruling power of the country; but very few ſubmit without reluctance to the mandates of ſubordinates. When military men, therefore, have had tranſactions only with the Board, your intentions have been cheerfully fulfilled: whereas, in all inſtances of inferior interference, ruinous diſſentions have been generated. Let me add, that the ſtrong enforcement of obedience by military trial, renders them more prompt and uſeful inſtruments of public duty, than thoſe of the other ſervice, who are under no control, and who, by hazarding an eventual but improbable diſmiſſion,

may

may commit repeated acts of diſobedience with impunity.

Thus far my obſervations have immediately referred to abuſes in your military ſyſtem; but what avails the improvement of that ſyſtem; which is only uſeful to protect your poſſeſſions, if waſte and devaſtation are ſuffered to render them hardly worth protecting, and unequal to ſupport the force on which their ſafety muſt depend? You have ſeen miſery in its worſt aſpect, the miſery of famine, abundantly predominant within the bound hedge of Madras: you have ſeen, under your own walls, the infant dying for want on the breaſt of his mother; the old and the young, the parents and the children, mingling their laſt groans, and expiring in your kennels: you have ſeen whole families of ſpectres in human ſhape, digging in the entrails of a dead carrion, and, when theſe means have failed, ſurrendering themſelves with a truly Aſiatic apathy to the wild dogs and vultures that waited to devour their carcaſes: you have ſeen, for months together, a hundred bodies daily covering your ſtreets, with circumſtances of horror too ſhocking to enumerate*! Nor is it within the bound hedge of Madras only, that the internal waſting of the country can be traced: during twenty-ſeven months of continued movement through a large extent of your dominions, the duties of my ſtation familiarized me with the whole gradation of territorial abuſes, neither leſs palpable nor diſtreſsful than thoſe with which you yourſelves are perſonally acquainted.

* Every practicable effort was made by Government and by individuals to relieve the diſtreſſes of the wretched natives, who flew from all quarters of the Carnatic to take ſhelter under the walls of Madras. Thouſands of them received daily diſtributions of rice, and many more were conducted, at the public expence, to the northern provinces, which had ſuffered leſs than the Carnatic by the calamities of war.

It

It has been already ſtated, that the ravages of the enemy are by no means the greateſt evils of which thoſe countries have complained. While the territorial management of the countries now aſſigned to the Company, remained with the Nabob, the oppreſſive practices undoubtedly prevailed that multiply exaction through every Eaſtern Government. Indefinite claims and arbitrary impoſitions fell heavy upon the Polygars, and other tributaries. The Head Renters and Amuldars of diſtricts, as well as all inferior inſtruments of collection, were impelled to haraſs the inhabitants, not only to ſatisfy their own rapaciouſneſs, but to feed the avarice of their ſuperiors; for they knew that the only tenure by which they held their appointments, was the frequent repetition of a bribe. The finances of the Durbar were involved by an unmethodized expenditure, and waſted on worthleſs Europeans at home and abroad. At length the diſburſements eſſential to the current buſineſs of the country were totally obſtructed, and the urgent claims of powerful individuals introduced the deſtructive practice of granting Tunkaws or aſſignments on particular diſtricts. In conſquence of which, the holder of the Tunkaw is veſted with the power of collecting the amount of his aſſignment within a certain ſpace and period by the moſt outrageous means.

A band of ill-regulated ſoldiery and burdenſome retainers conſumed the produce of the country, and diſturbed the labours of the farmer and manufacturer. Theſe cauſes of defalcation in the Nabob's reſources, at a moment when the exigencies of the late war demanded the utmoſt energy, afforded the ſtrong argument of urgent neceſſity for transferring his territory and revenues to the uſes and direction of the Company. The truth and juſtice of theſe arguments muſt of courſe remain, as long as the neceſſity on which they reſt.

At

At the ſame time it ſhould not be forgotten, that during the government of the Nabob, no European whatever, excepting thoſe in his ſervice, was permitted to have any influence in the country. The Engliſh, therefore, were exempted from the odium of perſonal interference, or rather the rod of Mooriſh deſpotiſm was contraſted with the milder attributes ſuppoſed to characteriſe an Engliſh adminiſtration.

When the Company aſſumed the ſovereignty, the transfer of authority from the eſtabliſhed ruler to an alien power, no doubt, impreſſed the natives with diſtruſt; in lieu of which your Committee of aſſigned revenue have, by their eminent exertions, ſubſtituted confidence and ſecurity. They have aboliſhed the deſtructive grants of Tunkaws, and other abuſes in the country management;—they have exhibited great ability, as well as unblemiſhed integrity;—and they have rendered the revenues extremely productive in most unprosperous times. It was not however possible for them entirely and immediately to repress the misconduct of inferior instruments*, who are eager to perpetuate oppression, and to enforce unusual measures by unprecedented means. The situation of the country rendered it necessary to continue the practice of renting extensive districts to the highest bidder: although every precaution was adopted to prevent the abuse of power, still the collections could not be enforced, unless an unrestrained authority were vested in the Renter. His object too frequently is, to take advantage of the present moment, and, doubtful of futurity in a country at all times liable to fluctuation, to ransack and embezzle, that he may go off at last enriched with the spoils of his province. The fact is, that in every part of the peninsula where the Renters are established, not only

* The Black agents, who manage the whole detail of collection in the different districts.

the

the Ryot and the husbandman, but the manufacturer, the artificer, and every other Indian inhabitant, is at the mercy of those ministers of public exaction*.

The established practice throughout this part of the peninsula has for ages been, to allow the farmer one half, of the produce of his crop, for the maintenance of his family and the recultivation of the land, while the other is appropriated to the Circar. In the richest soils under the Cowle of Hyder, producing three annual crops, it is hardly known that less than forty *per cent.* of the crop produced has been allotted to the husbandman: yet Renters on the coast have not scrupled to imprison reputable farmers, and to inflict on them extreme severity of punishment, for refusing to accept of sixteen in the hundred as the portion out of which they were to maintain a family,

* While Tinivelly remained under the superintendance of Mr. Irwin, that province formed an exception not less pleasing than exemplary from those general observations.

to

to furniſh ſtock and implements of huſbandry, cattle, ſeed, and all expences incident to the cultivation of their lands. But ſhould the unfortunate Ryot be forced to ſubmit on ſuch conditions, he has ſtill a long liſt of cruel impoſitions to endure:— he muſt labour weeks after weeks at the repair of water-courſes, tanks, and embankments of rivers;—his cattle, ſheep, and every other portion of his property is at the diſpoſal of the Renter, and his life might pay the forfeit of refuſal. Should he preſume to reap his harveſt when ripe, without a mandate from the Renter, whoſe Peons, Conicoplys, and Retainers attend on the occaſion, nothing ſhort of bodily torture and a confiſcation of the little that is left him could expiate the offence:— Would he ſell any part of his ſcanty portion, he cannot be permitted while the Circar has any to diſpoſe of:—Would he convey any thing to a diſtant market, he is ſtopped at every village by the Collectors of Sunkum or Gabelles, who exact a duty for

for every article exported, imported, or difpofed of. So unfupportable is this evil, that between Negapatam and Palagatcherry, not more than 300 miles, there are about thirty places of collection; or, in other words, a tax is levied every ten miles upon the produce of the country. Thus manufacture and commerce are expofed to difasters hardly lefs fevere than thofe which have occafioned the decline of cultivation.

But thefe form only a fmall part of the powers with which the Renter is invefted. He may fink or raife the exchange of fpecie at his own difcretion, he may prevent the fale of grain, or fell it at the moft exorbitant rates: thus at any time he may, and frequently does, occafion general famine. Befides maintaining a ufelefs rabble, whom he employs under the appellation of peons at the public expence; he may require any military force he finds neceffary for the bufinefs of oppreffion, and

and few inferior officers would have weight enough to juſtify their refuſal of ſuch aid. Should any one however diſpute thoſe powers, ſhould the military officers refuſe to proſtitute military ſervice to the diſtreſs of wretched individuals, or ſhould the civil Superintendant remonſtrate againſt ſuch abuſe, nothing could be more pleaſing to the Renter, who derives from thence innumerable arguments for non-performance of engagements, and for a long liſt of defalcations. But there are ſtill ſome other not leſs extraordinary conſtituents in the complex endowments of a Renter; he unites in his own perſon all the branches of judicial or civil authority, and if he happen to be a Bramin, he may alſo be termed the repreſentative of eccleſiaſtical juriſdiction. It would be impertinent to enlarge on the conſequences of thus huddling into the perſon of one wretched mercenary, all thoſe powers that ought to conſtitute the dignity and luſtre of ſupreme executive authority.

At the ſame time it is but juſtice to remark, that theſe obſervations cannot be with truth confined to the countries under Renters appointed in the countries belonging to the Nabob. The interior management and œconomy of Tanjore, in deſpite of the repreſentations of Mr. Sulivan and the exhortations of Mr. Swartz are ſtill more wretched. So wanton and iniquitous is the ſway of deſpotiſm there, that the goods of the merchant or carrier are frequently ſeized by order of the Durbar. If an individual native is incautious enough to diſplay his wealth, the Rajah's miniſters ſeldom reſt till he is caught and plundered: whips, ſcourges, thumb-ſcrews, and other inſtruments of Indian torture, are daily applied to the unhappy ſubjects in every Cutcherry, or court of juſtice, throughout the country. Every one therefore who poſſeſſes either gold or jewels, buries them in ſome ſecure ſpot, and entruſts the ſecret only to the moſt confiden-

tial

tial of his family. Hence almoſt the whole ſpecie of the country is diverted from the purpoſes of circulation; and an enormous annual loſs of treaſure is thus occaſioned by the frequent removal and extinction of families in that diſtracted territory. By theſe means the moſt fertile and once the moſt populous ſpot upon the globe, is already marked with the diſtinguiſhing features of a deſart.

If my information be not incorrect, a ſurvey of the Circars, or northern territory of Coromandel, would alſo exhibit a melancholy picture. Neither war nor convulſions have afflicted thoſe diſtricts for many years that they have been under the territorial adminiſtration of the Company, or of Zemindars dependant upon that authority. Their deſolation muſt therefore be ſtill more unequivocally imputed to internal miſmanagement.

When

When we recollect the original object of the English settlements in India, the benefits of a commercial intercourse with its once industrious coasts, we find that it has long ago been lost sight of in a multitude of territorial concerns, assumptions of sovereignty, and wanton extension of dominions which our situation renders us unfit to govern. Few of those who are employed in the Company's service will submit to the tedious drudgery of mercantile proceedings; they aspire at fortune through the more magnifying medium of contracts, paymasterships, residencies, and chiefships. The native merchants, Armenians, and others, who conducted the trading business of your Coast, have suffered so severely during the late distresses, as well as by the abolition of confidence and public credit, that they have removed to some less precarious situation, or else remain inactive in the hopes of better times. Neither would the present condi-

tion

tion of the Coaſt admit of any immediate means of re-eſtabliſhment from commercial exertions; for the ſtaple articles of your commerce are the produce of your lands, and the labours of the manufacturer: the decay and approaching extirpation of that uſeful claſs of ſubjects has been already traced. What then is to conſtitute the object of exportation? what is to yield the means of circulation, credit, and reſource? From the ſouthward you have at preſent no inveſtment*; in the Carnatic you have hardly the remains of former induſtry; in the Circars, hitherto undiſturbed by any foreign enemy, you find it difficult to load one annual ſhip for Europe. If the train of this induction be not falſe,

* Theſe obſervations concerning the decline of trade and the extirpation of manufacturers, muſt not be conſidered as entirely applicable to every ſpot upon the Coaſt. There are many villages to the ſouthward, and alſo to the northward, where there ſtill remains a ſufficiency of weavers to form an inveſtment if properly managed; and the French, as well as the Danes, have lately contrived to export conſiderable cargoes of Coaſt goods.

what hopes can you entertain of lightening the public embarraſſments, while every reſource in your Government is waſted?

Your predeceſſors left the country expiring under a complication of calamities. That your wiſdom and exertions ſhould have found means to prolong its exiſtence under ſuch a criſis, exceeded the expectations of your moſt ſanguine friends, and excites the admiration of your bittereſt opponents. You have already applied the firm hand of undeviating retrenchment to every branch of public expenditure, and labouring under unparalleled impediments, you have perſevered with a vigor and integrity of which there was no example in the Eaſt. By this conduct you may juſtly aſſume the merit of preſerving the Carnatic, oppreſſed with the formidable invaſion of native and European powers, and the more mortal wounds inflicted by the governments that preceded yours. But meritorious as retrenchment undoubtedly is, you feel the inefficiency of that alone to reſtore the public vigour. Fifty lacks of pagodas remain due by your Preſidency, for ſervices actually performed, or value received:—from that ſum, when audited, you cannot poſſibly make any diminution:—to attempt ſuch a meaſure would forfeit the whole character of Government, or at leaſt would be declaring the Indian Public inſolvent, and compelling their lawful creditors into a diſreputable compoſition. You have already heard the clamours excited by ſuppoſed injuſtice in the proſecution of œconomical reform. Too ſevere a retroſpect is not always beneficial, and in the preſent inſtance would prove deſtructive of equity and public faith. Perhaps it may be better to look forward; and inſtead of invalidating eſtabliſhed claims for paſt ſervices, to take care that every future charge ſhall accord with that juſt proportion which ſhould ever exiſt between the diſburſements and reſources of the treaſury.

Your debts, on their preſent footing, are deſtructive of all public welfare. With the wiſdom and vigour which have diſtinguiſhed your adminiſtration, if the Government were in any degree permanent, one year's revenue* of your country ought to equal their whole amount. Under a well-eſtabliſhed ſyſtem of public credit, ſo inconſiderable a proportional ſum, at the cloſe of a calamitous war, would hardly cauſe a perceptible inconvenience.——But conſider to whom, and in what manner this amount is due:—It has been incurred in a ſeries of five years of protracted and growing arrears, in all the fractions of pay, batta, extra-charges, and allowances to Civilians, Contractors, Soldiers, Sepoys,

* About fifty lacks of pagodas, or 2,000,000*l.*

Artificers, Camp-followers, and all defcriptions of men connected with the peace or war eftablifhment. If the unfortunate individual, urged by fevere neceffity, though he muft not hope for money, fhould demand a certified ftatement, he is haraffed with a long and fruitlefs attendance;—the auditor difputes his vouchers, and contefts his claims.——If at length the certificate fhould be granted, it remains an ufelefs docket; on the credit of which he can neither purchafe nor procure one fingle article of life. Your government has exhibited a political phenomenon, unprecedented in the annals of mankind——a ftate or public indebted almoft to every perfon in its fervice, and yet the functions of authority continuing unimpeded by any ferious commotion. Several circumftances however have fufficiently denoted the hazard of fuch a fituation. When the embarraffments refulting from a treafury exhaufted, a country defolate, and a credit ruined

ruined in the profecution of a deftructive war, impelled you to direct that all allowances of batta fhould ceafe, at a period when the arrears of the army and diftreffes of the country rendered that indulgence peculiarly indifpenfable, the remonftrances and vigorous meafures adopted by the military evinced the public danger of uniting the individuals of a community againft the Government. There is but one alternative;—you muft either liquidate the arrears due to your eftablifhment, or you muft rifk the lofs of India. If Europe and Bengal unwifely fhould withhold their aid, that liquidation cannot poffibly take place but by the re-eftablifhment of your own credit and finance: thefe, as well as commerce, are the offspring of cultivation and manufacture, which can exift only by induftry and population. Your endeavours to re-eftablifh that natural relation of things have already crowned the meafures of your adminiftration; and when carried to their full completion, will add, to the merit of having preserved the Carnatic from destruction, the distinguished character of having restored it to prosperity.

It would ill become me in addressing the Government of an extensive country, to enlarge on the detail of means by which this restoration may be effected. Permit me, however, to suggest, that the legislative, judicial and executive regulations necessary to the prosperity of an Indian Government are neither complicated nor refined. There is one maxim peculiarly applicable to that country,—that there is no evil more dreaded than innovation, nor any duty more sacred with the natives than custom. Let this truth then be the unalterable beacon and directory in all plans of renovation respecting India, where the continued repeals and fluctuations incident to European establishments excite the utmost dread and detestation.

The

The mode of reſtoring proſperity to your territories is, in my opinion, extremely ſimple. Theſe countries experienced the refinements of civil polity and regulation ſuited to their condition, ages before they even heard the name of European. You have only tc reſtore the general form and tenor of the Indian juriſprudence; and where that ſyſtem, over-rating the pretenſions of ſuperior caſts, tends to the violation of natural law and public welfare, there the rigour of Gentoo enactments ſhould be mitigated, without deſtroying the eſtabliſhed order and gradations of the country. Protect the poor from the oppreſſion of the great, reſtrain the deſpotic violence of the native leaders, and let every one within the limits of the Engliſh influence feel that he is ſafe in his property, his perſon, and his life. If this were actually the caſe, the huſbandman, the labourer, the manufacturer, and the merchant would very ſoon fly from every corner of Indoſ-

 tan,

tan, to take ſhelter under a government that reſpected the ſacred rights and eſtabliſhed inſtitutions of their anceſtors, while it afforded perſonal ſecurity and independence, the offspring of an Engliſh polity.

The country ſtill abounds ſo much with ſheep and cattle, that the full complement for all the purpoſes of labour and ſubſiſtence would ſoon be procured; the towns and villages would be repeopled, and the fields recultivated with a rapidity unknown in other climates. Such is the natural fertility of thoſe countries, and ſo ſtrong their propenſity to reproduction, that the quick renewal of abundance, induſtry, and commerce, is the neceſſary conſequence of ſecurity; which implies the protection of every one in the poſſeſſion of his own, by reſtraining all from the forcible or fraudulent appropriation of that which belongs not to themſelves. Neither is the celebrated Dr. Smith's remark leſs worthy of obſerv-

obſervance, that it is the height of impertinence, even for any public body, to interfere in the private concerns of individuals. How much more pernicious muſt the preſſure of that ſyſtem be, which delegates to every ſubordinate inſtrument of public authority, that privilege of individual interference, not for public welfare, but for ſelfiſh purpoſes at the expence of the property and induſtry of the ſubject!

While the company holds the territorial management of the country, it is to be dreaded that this happy renovation cannot be accompliſhed; becauſe your civil ſervants, by the conſtitution of your eſtabliſhment, are under no reſtraint, excepting thoſe of their own ſentiments. Every one knows that orders are nugatory where there is no puniſhment for diſobedience, and the ſevereſt denunciation of your diſpleaſure againſt a civil ſervant, only diſmiſſes him from a ſervice, which the very act that

incurs

incurs your cenſure probably enables and inclines him to relinquiſh. The expedient of military interference in the buſineſs of interior management, is ſtill a more egregious violation of all good policy and public truſt. For though military men are far more proper to be charged with ſpecific orders than Civilians, being anſwerable for diſobedience with their lives; yet the exertion of the military arm in the detail of civil regulation implies a total abrogation of all civil rights, and declares aloud that no power prevails but that of force.

You have already found, that ruinous as both theſe modes undoubtedly are, they ſeem mild and reputable, in compariſon with the only other means of management that it has hitherto been found practicable to adopt with ſucceſs in any part of India— the delegation of territorial authority to native Agents, and black Renters, who have

have no tie whatever of character, permanency, or situation to restrain them from the commission of outrages too atrocious for any European imagination to suggest. What then remains but to perform an act of equal policy and justice? To redeem the English name from the general imputation under which it labours, of violating the rights and honour of our best adherents, of coveting the possessions of friend and foe*, and of a total incapacity, from situation and constant change of system, to manage what we so unjustifiably acquire? Disprove the allegation, restore the country and the sovereignty to its

* The hardships and humiliation which have been endured by the Nabob of Arcot, by the Rajah of Tanjore, by the Nabob of Bengal, and by the Mogul himself, while under the protection of the English, afford the strongest grounds for other Princes of India to dread an intimate connexion with us. At the same time it must be confessed, that many powerful arguments may be adduced for retaining the interior management of the countries within our influence.

its rightful owner the Nabob*;—emancipate the Rajah of Tanjore, and all other Rajahs, Princes, and Zemindars, belonging to your Coaſt, from the vexatious interference of the civil, and from the rough aſſumptions of the military power;—employ the former in the proper duties of their ſtation, in the buſineſs of office and inveſtment; and in purſuance of your favourite ſyſtem of retrenchment, reduce their numbers to the proportional diminution of demand for their ſervices. Would they acquire fortune, let them aſpire to it, not in the ſpoils of diſtricts, but in the proſecution of commercial operation: as for the latter, confine them to their garriſons, ſtations, and cantonments; ſuffer them not to be ſcattered through the country, and remind them that their buſineſs is not uſury and exaction, but diſcipline and war. In

* This cannot be ſuppoſed to take place until the period for which the Nabob's revenues were aſſigned to the Company be elapſed, and until the object of that aſſignment be fulfilled.

order

order that this ſalutary alteration may be attended with popularity and effect, their profeſſional emoluments ought to be ſufficient, without any aid from indirect acquirement.

Should the Nabob, the Rajahs, or the Zemindars, take advantage of your indulgencies, and endeavour to withhold their ſtipulated payments; ſhew them that lenity and juſtice are neither the offspring of indolence nor weakneſs: but, on the firſt ſymptoms of their perſiſtance in ſuch delays, march a body of troops to enforce your orders, make them pay the expences of the expedition, and teach them that you will not ſuffer intentional miſconduct to paſs unpuniſhed. You have likewiſe to reſtrain every claſs of Europeans, the merchant only excepted, from mingling with the natives; for when they are familiariſed with our practices, they ceaſe to reſpect our virtues in the juſt abhorrence of our crimes.

Above

Above all, let it never be forgotten, that in the preſent ſtate of national depravity, wherever a latitude of power is lodged, whether in civil or military hands, the eye of juſtice muſt be more piercing, and her ſword more ſeverely pointed againſt delinquency, before you can hope to reſtrain the repetition of abuſe.

The reſtitution of the revenues and ſovereignty to the Nabob, will no doubt be oppoſed, on the former grounds of unwiſe and prodigal adminiſtration; aſſuredly, however, this evil may be remedied. You will alſo recollect, that the waſte and prodigality of the Durbar aroſe from the rapaciouſneſs of Europeans, who never ceaſed to prey upon the Nabob; but misfortune has fallen heavy on the hoary head of Mahomed Ally; the picture of European treachery is drawn in colours too ſtrong to be effaced from his remembrance. At any rate let him be removed from

from the Presidency, the chief seat of intrigue and corruption, and Europeans; let him be re-established in the ancient capital of his Government; let that capital be restored to its former splendor: he will there be rescued from the ruinous intercourse of powerful and designing adventurers, and the country will rejoice that there is again a rightful Sovereign.

But it will be asked, How shall you restrain the Nabob's Government from the detail of individual oppressions, arbitrary exactions, and frequent violations of the rights of property and persons, incident to all Asiatic institutions? To these let me answer, that the protection of the country, and an adequate appropriation of the revenues for the support of your establishment remaining in your hands, it becomes you to preserve a controlling authority sufficient to restrain abuse. The annual amount of sums due, services to be performed, rents to to be paid to the Circar, and groſs produce of every village, or Muganum on the Coaſt, have been accurately recorded for ages in the Cutcherries, or public Courts of the diſtricts. Should a Manager or Renter exact more than that ſtipulated or wonted ſum, refer to theſe records as the common and ſtatute law of the country, in all caſes of revenue: if the means of private admonition to the Durbar ſhould fail, let your Board or Government be the tribunal before which the cauſe is cogniſable in the laſt reſort; for it is preſumed that no inferior juriſdiction could give ſentence between the Nabob and his ſubjects. Should any ſervant of the Circar attempt to ſeize the property, or reſtrain the perſon of an inhabitant, let the injured party, if all inferior means of juſtice fail, have ultimate recourſe to the ſame ſuperior and controlling power: let the rulers and the ruled feel, that under the ſanction of an Engliſh Government, the poor as well as the rich are

are entitled to protection. It will leave nothing to be added to the merits of your Government, if you curb oppression, and cause the pure streams of English justice to unite with Indian jurisprudence, and both to flow in the channels of sacred, immemorial usage.

It must be confessed, that the power to restrain, implies also the power to commit abuse; and if such ministers of public vengeance as involved the Carnatic in the war with Hyder, were again to constitute the Government, it would be fruitless to suggest a thought of reformation. But this letter is addressed to a Board distinguished by rigorous and persevering integrity: we all know, that your minds cannot be swayed by any improper consideration; and that the animosity of party, though it may distract, has not been able to prevent your earnest endeavours for the public welfare. It may farther be presumed, that the attention of the nation is so awake to the state of India, that the succession to the Government in the different Presidencies will henceforth be composed of able and upright men; or else, that all expectation of preserving these settlements will for ever be relinquished.

Another circumstance is particularly deserving of consideration. It is a truth palpable to every mind at all acquainted with political œconomy, that no country whatever is more favourably situated for the support of public credit, and extensive circulation, than India. The mass of treasure has been so widely diffused, the avowed possession of private property is so insecure, and the mode of pecuniary transactions so disadvantageous, that any Government on whose integrity and stability the natives durst rely, might form the greatest bank of deposit on the globe. To the influence derivable from such an institution, would be added

the

the benefits of circulating bank or public ſecurities in lieu of ſpecie. Thoſe benefits are proportioned to the extent of country in which ſuch notes or ſecurities can have currency, to the quantity that may be ſafely iſſued, and to the length of time that they may remain in circulation, as well as to the gain derivable from the intermediate application of money, when not needed in the bank. The profit on bills of exchange, diſcounting bills, granting caſh accounts, and other operations of banking companies, are alſo conſiderable. In all theſe particulars, India poſſeſſes peculiar advantages: the range of circulation is more extenſive, the probable period of the notes returning into bank more diſtant, the rate of money higher, the tranſactions more numerous, and the profits on each tranſaction greater than in any other country. Had ſuch an eſtabliſhment of public ſecurity exiſted ſix years ago, your Preſidency could not have fallen into the ſtate

 of

of degradation which it has experienced; nor would it have been oppreſſed with a maſs of paltry debts, whoſe amount on their preſent footing may poſſibly overthrow the Government; but which, with the aid of ſuch a bank, could not for a moment have obſtructed the career of public ſervice. In that event, Hyder, ſo far from ravaging your country, and menacing you within the walls of Madras, would have been quickly driven from the Carnatic and from his own dominions.

Such an eſtabliſhment would attach all claſſes by the ties of private benefit; it would ſubject to your influence every prince in India, by enabling you to ſupply his wants, or to ſupport his adverſaries, according as his conduct merited your friendſhip or excited your reſentment. If ſimilar proceedings have exalted the Seets and other private Soucars throughout Indoſtan, to a weight and influence little ſhort of princely power, what might we not expect from the operation of such a machine, in the hands of a Government whose wisdom, justice, and stability, should entitle it to public confidence*?

If we might venture to suppose that these suggestions should ever grow into effect, we should no longer have occasion to dread the courts of India meditating our expulsion; for the adoption of a system formed on these principles implies such vigour of interior management, such encreasing opulence, such strictness in the detail of expenditure, such respectability of warlike preparation, and so direct a course of liberal policy towards all the country powers, as would either remove their enmity, or else evince their incapacity to subvert a fabric built upon so sure a basis.

* No degree of energy and rectitude in any individual Governor can possibly produce the benefits in question; it is the energy and rectitude of long established system alone, from whence they can be derived.

I have now, my Lord and Gentlemen, laid before you the condition of your ſouthern provinces, and the tenor of public proceedings ſince you honoured me with that command. After having ſtated fairly the embarraſſments under which we laboured, and the means employed to overcome them, I have dwelt with no leſs pleaſure than acknowledgment on the exertions of Mr. Sulivan and Mr. Irwin at the head of your ſouthern revenues, of Mr. Digby, Mr. Hippiſley, and Mr. Orpin, in other departments of civil ſervice; I have repeated the ſentiments of obligation due to Colonel Stuart, Colonel Forbes, and the other ſenior officers of the army, for the ſtrenuous ſupport received from them. It has alſo been my particular endeavour to impreſs your minds with a ſtrong and laſting ſenſe of the merits of your ſouthern troops, and I ſhall feel the higheſt ſatisfaction if my repreſentations ſhall procure for them

them any portion of your indulgence, due by indiſputable claims.

With regard to the obſervations ſubſequent to the narrative of thoſe proceedings in which the ſouthern army was engaged, they refer to the cauſes which occaſioned the decline of our affairs upon the Coaſt, and to the conduct that appears beſt ſuited to prevent a repetition of ſimilar diſaſters. Theſe conſiderations, and the motives which have induced me to ſubmit my opinion to your Honourable Board, will, I truſt, incline you to receive them with indulgence, as the well-intended ſuggeſtions of one whoſe zeal to promote the public ſervice exceeds either his abilities or opportunities of information on this complicated and important ſubject. Few perſons however have enjoyed more favourable occaſions of enquiry into the local circumſtances of thoſe territories; I am conſcious too, that my mind has neither been influenced by prejudice nor partiality. It only remains that I ſhould apologize for the tedious neſs of this addreſs, and repeat my warmeſt acknowledgments for the very flattering marks of public confidence which you were pleaſed to repoſe in me. Moſt cordially do I wiſh, as the beſt expreſſion of my gratitude, that the vigour, ability, and integrity of conduct by which your Preſident has been enabled to preſerve the countries under your direction, may procure to you the diſtinguiſhed honour of retrieving the Engliſh intereſts in the Eaſt.

I ſhall now take my leave of your Lordſhip and the Board, and bid adieu to the ſubject of India.

I have the honour to be, &c.

APPENDIX.

N° I.

Daraporam, 1ſt June 1783.

MY LORD, AND GENTLEMEN,

I Have the honour to inform your Lordſhip and the Board that the army encamped before this place on the thirtieth (afternoon), having made a march of twelve hours. We immediately inſpected the ground adjoining to the fort, and at three in the morning proceeded with ſome Euro-

Europeans and two battalions of Sepoys to take poſſeſſion of a very ſtrong poſt on the weſtern ſide of the river, within three hundred yards of the fort. The men were under cover before daylight; we opened a ſmall mortar battery at eight in the morning, a three gun battery before three in the afternoon, and effected a breach about ſix o'clock. Parties were ſent round the fort and pettah to prevent the eſcape of the enemy, who did not venture to ſtand a ſtorm, and the grenadiers entered at daybreak this morning.

We have ſpared the life of every perſon in the place, and have turned out all the lower claſs of people; but have thought it neceſſary to detain ſome of the principal inhabitants, in hopes of intelligence from them. It is a very extenſive place, and capable of much defence. I am happy to inform you, my Lord and Gentlemen, that there is a very conſiderable magazine of grain

grain in the fort and pettah, which might prove of eſſential conſequence in the execution of your orders for offenſive operations to the weſtward. A very large army might be ſubſiſted in this neighbourhood for a campaign: there is alſo a large ſupply of powder and ſhot in the magazines here. I ſhall have the honour to tranſmit a particular ſtate of the place, as ſoon as it can be prepared; and ſhall then take the liberty of ſubmitting to your conſideration my ideas of the eminent advantages that will reſult from the proſecution of your orders to the weſtward, provided you ſhall judge it expedient to ſend ſuch a reinforcement to this army as may enable us to ſecure ſome places of importance in the enemy's country, and at the ſame time to meet his army in the field. Should you, my Lord and Gentlemen, determine in favour of this meaſure, I may venture to aſſert that the conſequences will not be leſs beneficial than honourable: but in the preſent ſtate of this force, I cannot preſume to promiſe any permanent advantage.

I have, *&c.*

(Signed) W. FULLARTON.

The Right Hon. LORD MACARTNEY,
and the Select Committee, Fort St. George.

N° II.

Pandalamcourchy, 13th Aug. 1783.

MY LORD, AND GENTLEMEN,

IN anſwer to your Letter of the eighth of July, I had the honour on the nineteenth of July to inform your Lordſhip and the Honourable Board of my intention to proceed to Dindigul, in order to wait your farther commands in that place; and on the twenty-fifth and twenty-ſeventh of July the army marched in diviſions from Tritchinopoly by the route of Touracourchy; for there was not a ſufficiency of water by the ſhorter road of Manapar.

At Touracourchy I received a public letter from Mr. Sulivan, containing a formal requiſition that I ſhould move the army into the Mellore diſtricts, and from thence proceed

proceed myſelf with the detachment to Shevigunga, in order to enforce the payment of the tribute due in that country.

Your Lordſhip and the Honourable Board, in your Letter of the eighth of July, were pleaſed to give me a diſcretionary power of proceeding either to Dindigul or to any other place that might tend moſt effectually to enable this army to carry offenſive operations into execution, in the event of Tippoo's refuſing to accede to the terms of accommodation that have been offered to him. In addition therefore to the weight of Mr. Sulivan's arguments on this occaſion, and to the reſpect at all times due to his opinion, I conceived it to be my duty to comply with the requiſition in queſtion, as it did not interfere with any orders I had received, but on the contrary tended to promote every object of ſervice that this army could have in view.

We

We arrived at Mellore on the ſecond of Auguſt, and from thence proceeded to Shevigunga with an eſcort, whither two battalions were previouſly detached. On their approach, the Rajah and his Miniſters fled to the woods of Callacoil, and could not be prevailed upon to return; but in the courſe of four days I was lucky enough, in Mr. Sulivan's name, and with his ſanction, to bring them into an arrangement; of which Mr. Sulivan will communicate the particulars to your Lordſhip and the Board, and which I hope will meet with your approbation.

At Shevigunga I received a public Letter from Mr. Irwin, urging the movement of the army into the Tinivelly country, in order to repreſs the inſolence of the Polygars, and aſſuring me that by this movement he would be enabled to collect a very conſiderable ſum for the urgent neceſſity of the troops: about the ſame time I was informed

informed that the military ſtores preparing at Tanjore, and the detachment under Colonel Stuart, could not reach Dindigul ſooner than the twenty-fifth of Auguſt. I therefore, with the advice of Mr. Sulivan, determined to comply with Mr. Irwin's requiſition, and to employ the interval in procuring ſuch ſupplies for the army as might enable me to carry into execution any orders you may be pleaſed to give me.

I withdrew the troops from Shevigunga on the eighteenth, and joined the army at Trepatchetty. A battalion was left in Mellore, for the purpoſe of collection, and the remaining force marched by Pallamerry and Naiglapour to Pandalamcourchy, where we arrived yeſterday at two o'clock P. M. after marching eighty miles in four days*. The quickneſs of theſe marches had not given Catabomanaig time to return from

* The detachment from Shevigunga marched above one hundred miles in four days.

the

the ſiege of Chocumpetty; but we found in his fort about two thouſand armed men, who ſhut their gates, and manned their walls againſt us. I therefore reſolved to attack them immediately; for Catabomanaig was very ſoon expected himſelf, with eight thouſand men. We opened a four gun battery at four o'clock P. M. breached before ſeven, and, after a ſevere conteſt, took poſſeſſion during the night. Notwithſtanding the precautions that were taken, and the corps that we had ſtationed on the different faces of the fort, the troops were ſo fatigued that many of the enemy effected their eſcape. We have found about fourteen guns and a quantity of powder in the place, as well as ſome money, grain, and bullocks. The military ſtores ſhall be appropriated to the public ſervice, and the other articles diſtributed to the troops, or deſtroyed.

During the ſhort time we have to remain in this province, I ſhall uſe every effort to execute ſuch objects of ſervice as Mr. Irwin ſhall point out; for by doing ſo I have no doubt that the arrangements of the country will very ſoon be completed by his zeal and abilities, and that the army, which is already largely indebted to his exertions, will be amply ſupplied with money and means of conveyance, and enabled to reach Dindigul, as ſoon as the military ſtores at Tanjore and the detachment under Colonel Stuart, can arrive at that place.

I have now, my Lord and Gentlemen, laid before you the proceedings in which the army has been engaged ſince I had the honour of addreſſing you laſt. It will afford me the moſt ſincere ſatisfaction, if in theſe particulars my conduct ſhall merit your approbation, and in any degree tend to give effect to your intentions reſpecting the future operations of the ſouthern troops.

I have, *&c.*

(Signed) W. FULLARTON.

To the Right Hon. the Governor and Preſident, and the Select Committee, Fort St. George.

N° III.

Camp at Shevigerry, 3d Sept. 1783.

MY LORD, AND GENTLEMEN,

I Had the honour on the thirteenth of Auguſt to inform your Lordſhip and the Honourable Board, of the motives that induced me to move the army from Tritchinopoly to Pandalamcourchy, and of the reduction of that place. Since that time I have been conſtantly employed in uſing every effort in my power to bring the Polygars into proper terms of arrangement for their arrears, ſo as to enable Mr. Irwin to ſettle the affairs of this province to the advantage of the Company, and to ſupply the army with a ſufficient ſum for its intended operations. As the Polygars remained extremely dilatory, notwithſtanding the reduction of Pandalamcourchy, it was found neceſſary to march to this place, where the Shevigerry-chief was joined by Catabomanaig and two other Polygars, and had all together not leſs than ſix thouſand people. On the approach of the army they retired from the town of Shevigerry to the Comby; a ſtrong hold in the mountains, which never had been attacked, and which they conceived to be impregnable.

Mr. Irwin concurred with me in thinking that a reaſonable accommodation would be more for the Company's intereſt than to reduce the place by ſtorm. On this principle I remained four days in fruitleſs negotiation with theſe refractory Polygars, and even ſubmitted to truſt myſelf alone among them, in hopes of bringing their buſineſs to an amicable termination. But finding all my efforts ineffectual, I was under the neceſſity of uſing force.

The Comby is ſituated in the receſs of an amphitheatre of very high rocks and mountains,

tains, and defended in front by a very ſtrong work, mounting eight guns, and covered by four miles of thick jungle, interſected with barriers and ravines; the whole being incloſed from the country with a high embankment.

The attack commenced yeſterday morning at ſeven o'clock. We were ſo fortunate as to carry the bank, which the enemy had lined with many thouſand men, and to drive them into the woods: we then proceeded to cut a road through the jungle, and effected this ſervice in ſeven hours, under a continual fire of muſketry and repeated ſallies of the enemy, who were ſeldom farther from our front than thirty or forty yards, and ſeveral times ruſhed upon our people with their pikes, but were as often repulſed. As ſoon as we had forced our way to the foot of the high mountain that commands the Comby to the ſouthward, we advanced to

 gain

gain the ſummit, and by ſix o'clock we had driven the enemy from their poſts upon the eminence; and from thence we kept up ſuch a fire upon the Comby that they were forced to abandon the place, and to retreat through rocks and thickets, where it was impoſſible for us to purſue them with any effect: we have found eight guns, three elephants, and a large quantity of grain. I cannot ſay too much in commendation of the officers and men in this buſineſs; and am happy to add, that if we conſider the ſtrength of the place, our loſs is extremely inconſiderable, as will appear from the encloſed copy of the killed and wounded.

I am in hopes, my Lord and Gentlemen, that this ſucceſs will bring all the Polygars into an immediate arrangement with Mr. Irwin; for the letter of the eighth of Auguſt which I have juſt received from your Lordſhip and the Honourable Board, and

and the approach of the detachment under Colonel Elphinſton towards Tritchinopoly, renders it impoſſible for me to think of remaining any longer in this quarter; and I ſhall in conſequence move the army immediately to Dindigul, in order to carry forward thoſe important operations which you have been pleaſed to direct me to purſue from thence.

I ſhall think myſelf particularly fortunate if my movement to the Tinivelly country, and the operations that have taken place ſince my arrival, ſhall be honoured with your approbation, and tend to give effect to your expectation from the Southward.

I have, *&c.*

(Signed) W. FULLARTON.

To the Right Hon. the Governor and Preſident, and the Select Committee, Fort St. George.

N° IV.

Fort of Palagatcherry, 15th Nov. 1783.

MY LORD, AND GENTLEMEN,

I Had the honour on the eighteenth of October to inform your Lordſhip and the Honourable Board, that I had received official information from Tellicherry of a breach of faith, and a recommencement of hoſtility on the part of Tippoo Saib, againſt Mangalore. The critical ſituation of that important place, and the tenor of my inſtructions, induced me to move towards Palagatcherry, in order to reduce a fort of ſuch eſſential conſequence to the Engliſh intereſts in India, and at the ſame time to produce, if poſſible, a diverſion in favour of Mangalore.

After various difficulties in cutting our way near twenty miles through the foreſt of of Annamally (a jungle till then considered as impenetrable for an army), the advance of the line reached this place on the second of November; but the badness of the roads and incessant rains prevented the rear of the army with the battering guns from arriving till the ninth. I found the fort covered by a respectable glacis with a good covert way, a very broad and deep ditch completely reveted, a large berme, and a very strong commanding rampart. The figure of this fort is nearly quadrangular, the dimensions of its faces are 528 feet by 432; each angle is defended by a capacious round bastion with seven or nine embrasures, and a bastion of a similar construction on the centre of each curtain; it has only one entrance, passing through three gateways, mounts twenty-nine guns on the works, and contained a garrison of near four thousand men.

On

On the thirteenth, we opened two batteries of ſix heavy guns each, one on the eaſt and the other on the north face;—the enemy's fire was ſoon ſilenced, and their defences deſtroyed. At night, Captain Maitland, with a part of the four flank battalions under his command, took advantage of a heavy rain to drive the beſieged from the covert way. He was ſo fortunate as to ſucceed, and purſued them within the firſt and as far as the ſecond gateway; there he was ſtopped; but maintained his ground with great ſpirit and ability, until an addition of troops arrived. The enemy was ſo much alarmed with this mode of attack, that they called out for quarter, and put us in poſſeſſion of a fort capable of making a long and deſperate reſiſtance.

We have found 50,000 pagodas in the place, beſides a conſiderable ſtock of grain, powder, ſhot, and military ſtores; returns of of these articles, together with an accurate plan of the fort, and of the attack, shall be transmitted as soon as they can possibly be prepared; in the mean while a section of the north face is enclosed. Our loss on the occasion was extremely inconsiderable, as you will perceive by the annexed return of killed and wounded.

I have been minute, my Lord and Gentlemen, in the description of this place, because its consequence and local situation are not accurately known to Europeans. The possession of it commands a fertile and extensive district, the adjacent forests abound with the finest teek timber in India, and the river of Paniani is at hand to float it to the Malabar sea. The position of this place equally menaces the possessions of Tippoo on the western coast and towards Mysore, by the route of Coimbatour and Gudgereddy. The movements of this army, almost without money, conveyance, or or ſubſiſtence, except what we procured on our progreſs, afford ſufficient proof that magazines of grain eſtabliſhed here would enable armies to march with confidence and ſecurity from the coaſt of Coromandel to that of Malabar, and thus bring the military reſources of Madras and Bombay into one point of union and effect.

I have ſet the Killidar and the garriſon at liberty, with their ſide arms and private baggage, and am uſing every effort to put the place into the beſt ſtate of defence, as well as to prepare every department of the army for more important operations; as I am very lately informed by Brigadier General Macleod, that Tippoo Saib is ſtill blockading Mangalore, and is determined if poſſible to reduce it. This has induced the Preſidency of Bombay to give orders that General Macleod ſhall uſe every effort to ſave that important fortreſs. I have the honour to forward a letter from General

neral Macleod to the Right Honourable the Prefident on this fubject.

The Rajah of Calicut, or reprefentative of the ancient Zamorins, is now with me, and we receive much affiftance from the Bramins and other inhabitants of this country, on whom I beftow every mark of favour and protection, in order as much as in my power to preferve the Englifh name from the ftain too often incurred by violence and oppreffion: I have likewife received the ftrongeft affurance of friendfhip and fupport from the different Rajahs on the Malabar coaft. I have written to Sir Edward Hughes, to Brigadier General Macleod, and to the Chief of Tellicherry, foliciting moft earneftly a fupply of battering guns, powder, fhot, and other military ftores, which could eafily be fent to me by the route of Calicut. Should thefe requifitions be complied with, and the war with Tippoo

poo be continued, I have little doubt of being able to march to Seringapatam in hopes of deciding this destructive contest at the gates of his capital. But should your Lordship and the Honourable Board decide on measures of immediate pacification, and wish to preserve possession of the country between this place and Tritchinopoly, it is easily within my power to fulfil these views, by falling back to Coimbatour and Erode; for these places, in addition to the country already reduced, would add a revenue of 790,000*l.* per annum, and extend the English territory almost entirely across the peninsula.

The very pressing necessities of the officers and troops have obliged me to take upon myself to order a distribution of the money found in the fort, which I am aware is a measure that may possibly involve me in personal inconvenience; but which I presume no person will venture to attribute

to

to any private conſideration, when it is explained that I have not, on my own account, received nor ſtated any charge to the public ſince my arrival in India; but am applying to the exigencies of the ſervice every fraction I can either borrow or procure.

I have already informed your Lordſhip and the Honourable Board of the very ſpirited conduct by which Captain Maitland of the ſeventy-eighth regiment accelerated the fall of the place. The exertions of Lieutenant Colonel Kelly, during the courſe of the attack, claim my warmeſt thanks. Lieutenant Colonel Elphinſtone was field-officer of the trenches on the night of the thirteenth, and conducted the operations in a manner worthy of his long ſervice and high military character. It would be difficult for me to do juſtice to the merits of Colonel Stuart and Colonel Forbes, on this and every other occaſion.

Captain Byres the chief engineer is entitled to my beſt thanks for his labours and ability.

I have, &c.

(Signed) W. FULLARTON.

To the Right Hon. the Preſident and Governor, and Select Committee, Fort St. George.

N° V.

Camp at Dindigul, April 26th, 1784.

MY LORD, AND GENTLEMEN,

IN obedience to your orders of the fifteenth of April, I have confidered with the utmoft attention the important objects held forth by your Lordfhip and the Board; and I beg leave to affure you of my beft efforts to fuggeft and to promote fuch meafures and arrangements as may tend moft effectually to eftablifh a permanent fyftem of protection and defence throughout the fouthern countries, to reduce as much as may be practicable the military expences of the fouthern eftablifhment, and to enable the army to affemble and to move with effect on any emergency. Thefe I conceive to be the effential points on which you direct me to lay my sentiments before you.

With respect to the allotment of troops for the different garrisons to the southward, I presume that two complete battalions in Tanjore, and one in each of the forts of Tritchinopoly, Madura, Palamcottah, Râmnad, and Kalicoil, including Tripatore, will be sufficient for the ordinary duties of the place.

It is not in my power at present to consult with Mr. Sulivan and Mr. Irwin on the proportion of troops that they may judge necessary for the collection of revenue in the different districts; I must therefore beg leave to refer in this particular to the opinions which they may transmit to your Lordship and the Board. Should Mr. Sulivan state that the four or five battalions of Tanjore Sebbendies are adequate to the purpose of collection in that country; and should

ſhould Mr. Irwin be ſatisfied with two battalions for the current tranſactions of the provinces under his management; it will next remain to be conſidered what Sepoy force in cantonment will enſure the ſafety and defence of theſe extenſive territories. It muſt not be forgotten that the countries of Tritchinopoly, Madura, Tinivelly, and Marawa, contain above one hundred thouſand Colleries and Polygars in arms, naturally brave, and habitually impatient of all regular government.

The Engliſh poſſeſſions and reſources to the ſouthward have been ſo recently endangered and impaired by the rebellious ſpirit of theſe ſavages, that I ſhall never preſume to be reſponſible for the efficacy of any arrangement of defence, until the moſt refractory of them are diſarmed, their woods and ſtrong holds laid open, and their forts occupied on the very firſt appearance of diſobedience, or diſreſpect to the Circar.

In conjunction with this primary measure of security, I have no doubt that six battalions of Sepoys, cantoned with an efficient force of Europeans near Tritchinopoly, and ready to be detached as occasion might require, would fulfil every public purpose that could occur within the provinces. Here I must observe, that many eminent advantages will arise to the service from this proposed mode of answering all requisitions for troops by detachments from the cantonments, instead of appointing battalions to permanent stations, which impairs their discipline, and is productive of various inconveniencies.

Considering the public interests no farther than as internal and defensive arrangements are in question, it will appear to your Lordship and the Board by this statement, together with the enclosed return of regular and irregular corps serving south of the Coleroon, that four battalions, including the detach-

detachments of the twelfth and eighteenth, can be withdrawn from hence, and that a body of Mogulleys, Independents, Irregulars, and troops belonging to His Highneſs the Nabob, amounting to ten thouſand men, may be immediately reduced: ſuch horſes of the Mogulleys as are fit for duty might be purchaſed for the regular cavalry, and the horſemen, who are in general men of high caſts and long ſervice, may be provided for in ſuch manner as may ſeem beſt to your Lordſhip and the Board.

A proportion of the Independents, Irregulars, and Nabob's troops, might be enliſted, or draughted into the regular battalions, and their black officers permitted to remain as ſupernumeraries on the ſtrength of theſe corps. Thus the hardſhips that would befal the individuals by reduction may be obviated, and the regular battalions which have ſuffered ſo ſeverely during the

 late

late conteſt may be effectually recruited, even to the preſent war eſtabliſhment of one thouſand men for each battalion: from this reduction alone, excluſive of the retrenchment of all field-allowances, an expenditure of more than twenty-five or thirty thouſand pagodas per month may be ſaved to the Company.

Were theſe arrangements to take place, a rigid ſyſtem of diſcipline to be maintained among the troops, the decayed parts of the principal forts to be repaired, and particularly a conſtant and ſcrupulous attention to be paid to the ſtate of grain, ſtores, ordnance, and ammunition in the different garriſons, I ſhould preſume that little would ſeem wanting to the well-being of the provinces, as far as the military are concerned, provided a ſufficient fund was appropriated to the ſpeedy diſcharge of the large arrears ſo long due to the troops, who have fought patiently

tiently and bravely under an accumulation of difficulties. I muſt farther beg leave to obſerve, that in my opinion nothing ſhort of ſuch a proviſion can ſecure to us the confidence of the Sepoys, on whoſe adherence and attachment our permanency in this country muſt ultimately depend.

Your Lordſhip and the Board are ſo fully impreſſed with the neceſſity of dedicating the moments of peace to the purpoſes of preparation, in order to guard againſt the uncertainty of future events, that I cannot fulfil the duty you have impoſed upon me without ſome obſervations on the mode by which the ſouthern troops may be enabled to aſſemble and to move as an army, whenever a renewal of hoſtility ſhall render that meaſure neceſſary.

If it ſhould appear to your Lordſhip and the Board, as it does to me, that there is not any place on the coaſt of Coromandel from

from whence an army could commence its operations with more advantage against the Mysoreans, or indeed against the French at Pondicherry, than from Tritchinopoly, that garrison will naturally become the repository of all the field and battering train, ammunition, and stores of every denomination, necessary to equip an army for the field: and, for the same reason, as well as for the convenience of the troops to be cantoned in its vicinity, a very ample magazine of grain and other provisions should be formed there; but the determination of the Renter to counteract any measure of this nature will require the most positive orders from your Lordship and the Board to give it effect.

In order that the troops in cantonment may at all times be ready to move, I conceive that every Captain commanding a battalion should be directed to entertain, at the usual allowances, a number of draught and

and carriage bullocks, complete with maſtries, drivers, gunney-bags, noſe-ropes and ſaddles, agreeably to the proportions ſpecified in the regulations for the conveyance of the brigade of guns, and their tumbrils, the tents, ſtores, and ammunition belonging to his corps; ſome gun and tent Laſcars and artificers ought alſo to be attached to the battalions; and a ſum might be allowed to the officers for furniſhing and repairing their own tents, which would greatly relieve the embarraſſments of public conveyance in the army: but ſhould any officer ever abuſe theſe indulgencies, a court martial and diſmiſſion from the ſervice would ſoon remedy the evil. A corps of artillery, complete in Europeans, Gulandars, and Laſcars, under the ſenior officer of artillery to the ſouthward, and a proportion of draught and carriage bullocks for the field and battering train, artificers belonging to the Commiſſary of Stores department, Dooly Coolies, and public followers

lowers of all descriptions, sufficient to equip the army, according to the strength you intend it to consist of, should constantly be complete in the cantonments: and as well as the bullocks thus proposed to be maintained upon the peace establishment, these followers may be occasionally employed in the carriage of grain and other business of the Circar, on requisition from the senior civil servant of the station, taking care always that the bullocks shall be attended by a guard of the corps to which they are attached. I also conceive, that a corps of pioneers, under the chief engineer, is extremely necessary to remain upon the establishment.

The expence attending cavalry, and the difficulty of procuring an efficient body of them, almost preclude me from any observations on that subject; but if it be your intention to complete that essential constituent of an army, I shall be happy

to

to have your instructions to procure horses from Mysore and other places; and at all events I flatter myself that you will judge it expedient to encrease, and to form into one regiment, the three troops of regular horse now serving to the southward.

Should these arrangements take place, implying a reduction of ten thousand men, and a removal of four regular battalions from hence, it would be necessary, on the renewal of hostility, to reinforce this side of the Coleroon with a force equal to that now supposed to be withdrawn, and to order an additional body of troops to be raised for the purpose of country duty and collection; otherwise it would be impossible to render the southern army at all equal to its present strength: but in this event, it will prove of eminent utility to raise regular corps in preference to the rabble of Peons, Independents, Fynauts, and other idlers, who infest the country, disgust the Sepoys, and impede the recruiting of the battalions.

With

With theſe precautions, my Lord and Gentlemen, I cannot think that any Indian enemy could ever gain ſuch advantages over us as have, on a late occaſion, endangered the exiſtence of the Engliſh in the Eaſt; for it is evinced by ſevere experience, that a number of troops alone is of little avail, unleſs the means, conveyance, and departments that conſtitute the eſſentials of an army, are maintained on ſuch a footing of effect as your Lordſhip and the Board ſeem determined to eſtabliſh.

I ſend this Letter to Mr. Sulivan, that he may forward it with his remarks and emendations. I ſhall only farther entreat your indulgence for the tediouſneſs of this detail.

I have, *&c.*

(Signed) W. FULLARTON.

To the Right Hon. LORD MACARTNEY, K. B.
Governor, Preſident, and Select Committee,
Fort St. George.

N° VI.

A particular Account of the Tanjore Country, and of its Produce.

THE Yacojee Rajah was the firſt man who took poſſeſſion of the fort and country of Tanjore from a Gentoo king; this event happened on the 7th day of February 1675, dated, in Gentoo, Rauchina Nama Sum vacharum, Magah Sudda Septinee. It appears, from the books which are kept in the palace, that there were 5753 villages, which ſaid villages were divided into the five following ſubahs or diſtricts; *viz.*

Subah Trivady,
Subah Combeconum,
Subah Mayaveram,

Subah

Subah Munnargoody,
Subah Pattacotah and Valumputt.

The country produced, in the year 1675, under the Yacojee Rajah, Paddy Cullums	32,050,000
Yacojee's eldeſt ſon Shahajee ſucceeded to the government; and the country yielded annually, during a reign of thirty-ſix years, Paddy Cullums	32,050,000
Shahajee was ſucceeded by his brother Sharabajee, who held the government eighteen years; the country produced annually — —	24,000,000
This deficiency in the revenue was attributed to the careleſſneſs of his manager.	
Tuccojee ſucceeded his brother Sharabajee, and reigned ſix years; the produce of the country was annually	24,000,000

Tuccajee was succeeded by his ſon Baba Saib, who lived one year; the lands produced, Paddy Cullums ——	20,000,000
At his deceaſe, his wiſe Surjana took charge of the government for two years; and the produce was, *per annum*,	20,000,000
At her death the ſon of Sharabajee (called Colerajah) ſucceeded to the government for one year; the produce was	20,000,000
And Colerajah's ſucceſſor was Pretab Sing, youngeſt ſon of the deceaſed Tuccojee; he enjoyed the government twenty-four years and a half; his four managers were Annajee Shanjogee, Ragupaty a Yangare, Manajee and the Dobeer; under theſe four managers the country produced every year	17,000,000

Pretab Sing's eldeſt ſon Tuljajee Maharajah ſucceeded to the throne; he employed the undermentioned managers; *viz.* Manojee Huſſain Cawn, Surerow Balajee Sinda, Dobeer Giligiliaha, Bachanna Hircar Rangia; the country produced, under theſe managers, every year, Paddy Cullums — 15,000,000

Some time after this, the Nabob took poſſeſſion of the country and fort of Tanjore; he appointed the Dobeer to be the ſole manager, under whoſe management the country produced — —— 17,000,000

As ſoon as the Rajah was reſtored to his fort and country he appointed Bachana Saula Vencataputty Tondamanapa, Annabochy Naick, Gillanapa, Hircar Rangia; under theſe managers the country annually yielded — — 15,000,000

The two last years, I believe, it has fallen as low as 13,000,000.

N. B. The foregoing account was received from an old man, who was a writer under the Dubeer and Manojee in the time of Pretab Sing, father to the present Rajah of Tanjore. It is given literally from the Mahratta Translation.

An Account of the Tanjore Revenues, extracted from the Circar Books in the three laſt Years of the Rajah's Father's Reign; viz.

In the year 1759 — 32 lack of Chuckrums.
1760 — 33 D°
1761 — 37 D°

In the two firſt years of the preſent Rajah's adminiſtration, in the year 1762 — 28 D°
1763 — 33 D°

1771, being the year of the firſt ſiege of Tanjore, 34½ lack of Chuckrums.

During the Nabob's government in the year 1773 — 33½ D°
1774 — 52 D°

1775, being the year of the Rajah's reſtoration, the Nabob received, during the

the time the country was poſſeſſed by him,
20 lack of Chuckrums.

The Rajah received, in the remainder of that year,	10	D°
Loſt by a change of government	10	D°
In the year 1776 —	26	D°
1777 —	24	D°

THE END.

ERRATA.

Page 25. —— 9. *for* againſt *read* to.
37. —— 9. *for* renovation *read* reformation.
49. —— 3. *for* ſeries *read* ſyſtem.
52. —— 12. *for* by their uſage *read* by their ill uſage.
70. —— 19. *for* yet conceived *read* conceived yet.
77. —— 4, *Note*; *after* buſineſs *add* of the ſervice.
149. —— 9. *after* ſeveral *add* hundred.

In the Plate of the Order of Battle, for C. Ebert *read* C. Everett.